EVERYT... YOU NEED T... TO WIN

THE LONG WAR
& COMMON CORE

*An exposé of the
totalitarian takeover of education
and America's loss of liberty.*

> *To make them love [servitude] is the
> task assigned to ... schoolteachers.*
>
> Aldous Huxley, *Brave New World*

Donna H. Hearne

THE LONG WAR AND COMMON CORE

FIRST EDITION

Cover art by Gerald E. Coleman.

Quantity discounts available from The Constitutional Coalition, PO Box 37054, St. Louis, Missouri 63141.

Published by Freedom Basics Press, PO Box 37054 St. Louis, MO 63141

ISBN 978-0-692-38933-1

ACKNOWLEDGEMENTS

This book has been a labor of love by more than the author. Walking along side have been several indispensable co-laborers. Landreth Johnson, who helped to do the layouts, editing and graphics of the first books we published in the 1990s, has lent her magical touch once again. Susan Merrick, whose critical eye, enthusiasm, wisdom and sense of humor, helped take a complex, lengthy manuscript of hundreds of pages and make it more understandable. Stanley Reahard brought time and the seasoned editorial eye with questions and suggestions, again helping to take thirty years of research and make it readable.

Most important is my husband, Mark, who has given necessary critiques and wise suggestions through the years. He has always been there and is forever my rock. There are others, too many to list, who believed in this project with encouragement, motivation, and prayers. Some have even underwritten a portion of the project. They helped to make this happen, and I am indebted to their faithfulness.

Those that know me, know that the reason I accepted this challenge came because of my morning quiet times with my Creator, Savior God who kept me on task with great excitement, joy and many blessings. Then, as I looked into the faces of my fifteen grandchildren, who will have to live in this world we adults have created for them, I knew that I could not stop.

May our efforts help provide the means to reverse this *long war* against liberty and freedom, and open enough eyes to make the difference. May America once again be blessed with moral certitude, intelligent independent thinkers, and creative optimistic leadership who recognize tyranny and have a passionate understanding of liberty and freedom.

May we once again be
"one nation under God with
liberty and justice for all."

TABLE OF CONTENTS

PREFACE

I n 1981, I was asked by President Ronald Reagan to serve in the U.S. Department of Education in a policy making position focusing on research and information. Although a certified elementary school teacher, I was little prepared for what my colleagues and I uncovered as we delved into the *heart of the beast*. My first task was to certify to the president what was happening in educational research and development. Refusing to rubber stamp what the Carter administration had done, I (along with several others) started to ask questions and explored under-the-radar research laboratories and centers. What we discovered was the *long war,* as spelled out in this book.

We uncovered amazing documents unknown to parents who were connected with their schools, dedicated teachers and good competent administrators. This was the beginning of thirty-plus years of research, and in the 1990s, resulted in the publication of three straightforward books: *The Dawning of the Brave New World; Sex, School and Politics;* and *Paychecks and Power* written in an effort to awaken America's families to the coming and ultimate collision of the individual and the state. *The Long War and Common Core* is birthed from these three works, along with a culmination of articles from *Front Line,*[1] a journal of current public policy information published by The Constitutional Coalition, and other resources.

M y last appointment (1988) from the Reagan White House was to the executive board of what was then called "America 2000." The executive board included me, one other person from the White House, and sitting governors and U.S. Senators. Governor Bill Clinton was in charge, and from 1986-1987 he served as chairman of the National Governors Association, was a leader of the education task force of the NGA and responsible for getting the project under way. Governor Clinton punted, focusing on what became the foundational agreement for a revolution in education – the summit in Charlottesville, Virginia, September 27-28, 1989. Alyson Klein, *Education Week*, discussed this historic summit quoting former New Jersey Governor Thomas H. Kean who said, "The Common Core is a descendant of Charlottesville and its aftermath."[2] My job assignment from President Reagan was to *push back* against the federal takeover of education. Although I never had the chance in that venue to do so, this book is the result of a lifetime of *push back*, and for the first time in thirty years, I can see light at the end of the tunnel.

My hope? The primary place for passing on freedom is through family, church, and the classroom. As you will see, the enemies of freedom well understand this, while the American people, content in their own world of personal peace and affluence, have been unaware of the *long war* against freedom. *The good news?* The advent of Common Core math, pornographic literature, and "anti-American" American history is awakening the great mainstream. By learning the facts, understanding the fault lines, and learning where and how to *push back*, Americans have a chance to again live their lives free of government propaganda and oppression, ready to pass on the wonders of America to the next generation through schools that reflect mainstream values. *And, take back the souls and minds of our children.*

By understanding the threats to freedom as well as how to re-establish the strengths of freedom and liberty in the culture and schools, the future can be better because the ideas taught in the schools become public policy. Working together, the future can be one of fewer taxes, less regulation, stronger intact families, and a society where not only has crime been reduced and economic prosperity widely enjoyed, but we can protect ourselves against foreign threats such as Shariah/Islamic/Jihadists. By taking back control of the schools and reintroducing the traditional curriculums, the worldview and understandings of freedom and liberty that our Founding Fathers embraced, we can change our nation. **But** we need to move beyond the false premise of moral relevancy and take a stand for those absolutes proven through the centuries. Together, we can begin a dialog about what **can** be done in a divided America to unite the generations and nationalities that make up America. We need the American people to engage.

The two **most powerful phrases** in recorded history are:

We hold these Truths to be self-evident, that all Men are created equal, that they are endowed by their Creator with certain unalienable Rights, that among these are Life, Liberty, and the Pursuit of Happiness ... (U.S. Declaration of Independence), and

So God created mankind in His own image. (Genesis 1:27)

These two phrases liberated mankind, giving him eternal, unconditional value and purpose within the framework of a nation that recognized all human life as of equal value. These two phrases together, freed him from tyrannical government's claim that each of us only has value and purpose as long as we are servants of the state. This is what the American Revolution was really about. Common Core seeks to banish not only these phrases, but also the rightful understanding of them. For freedom to endure, Americans **must** understand and embrace this distinctiveness of America. **Human life is sacred.**

But first, we must understand this *long war* against *freedom*.

INTRODUCTION

Across America moms and dads are struggling to help their children complete homework that frequently brings the student and sometimes the parents to tears. How would you help your grade school child solve this homework multiplication problem?

Multiply 164 times 72.

Common Core Math Uses:

LATTICE METHOD

```
      1   6   4
   1 0╱4 ╱2 ╱8  7
    ╱7 ╱2 ╱8
   1 0╱2 ╱1 ╱0  2
    ╱2 ╱2 ╱8
      8   0   8
```

OR

PARTIAL PRODUCTS METHOD

```
   164    164     64      64      64      64
 x  72  x  72  x  72  x   72  x   72  x   72
            8       8       8       8    1  8
          120     120     120     120
                  200     200     200
                  280     280     280
                         4200    4200
                        +7000   +7000
                                11,808
```

Traditional Math Uses:

The performance of the Lattice and Partial Products Methods do not make sense to you, because you remember being taught to use the Standard Algorithm Method[1]:

STANDARD ALGORITHM METHOD

```
       164
     x  72
       328
      1148
     11,808
```

As you sit with your child trying to help, your first response might be that it is stupid to make something as simple as compound multiplication take so many steps and consume valuable time and space needed to lay down the knowledge base of arithmetic necessary before moving on to algebra. There are only so many hours in a week to learn the basics of arithmetic.

Another evening at the dinner table, your ninth grade child tells you how he is embarrassed over a reading assignment. You take a look at what has been suggested for English Common Core and are aghast that your child is being exposed to passages clearly intent upon removing their modesty and moral inhibitions against pre-marital sex. You go to the Internet and find that in Newburgh, New York, teachers complained at a Board of Education meeting about the book, titled *Black Swan Green*. "One English teacher told the board, 'At least three of the books listed on the [New York State Common Core curriculum] contain passages using inappropriate language and visual imagery that most people would consider pornographic.' "[2] This sexually-explicit book is listed as a Common Core exemplar. *Black Swan Green* by David Mitchell, contains passages that 9th-graders study where a 13-year-old boy describes his father's genitals, as well as a sex act.

Your eleventh grade high schooler, not to be left out of the discussion, tells you about the Advanced Placement American History worksheets that have *somehow* left out the Thomas Edisons, Benjamin Franklins, and the rich history of George Washington in favor of social justice. Gone is American exceptionalism. Where are the heroes of liberty? Instead, the AP worksheets focus on the racial, native American, and gender "injustices" of America and the sense of entitlement to those who have been singled out as victims.

Finally, you discuss your concerns with fellow parents and find much more. Across the United States, Islamic indoctrination is occurring as the schools follow Common Core texts that glorify Islam but ignore, even

American students 1930 ... American students 2013

demonize, Christianity.[3] Young women are made to wear burqas and told that Muslim terrorists are actually *freedom fighters*.[4] One mom tells you of an "official *Hijab Day* in cooperation with Hamas-linked CAIR."[5] A flier was distributed that "shows that another Muslim Brotherhood-linked organization, the Muslim Students Association, is also involved. Every female member of the faculty and staff, and students as well, has been encouraged to wear a hijab today."[6] The flier read, "January 28, 2015 – The hijab is a headcovering worn by Muslim women as a symbol of modesty and their devotion to god. Girls! Come to the library Wednesday morning and MSA [Muslim Student Association] members will assist you in putting your hijab on. You can bring ANY type of rectangular (or square) scarf that is bought at any store (If you do not have any scarves, they will be provided for you to borrow for the day.)"[7]

A few nights later, you turn on TV's nightly news where the first ten minutes list the latest killings, beatings and destruction of your fellow human beings. You also see the recent videos of ISIS executing and slaughtering innocent people. It seems outlandish, but is it all connected? Why is this happening and what can be done about it?

T*he Long War and Common Core* is a comprehensive history of Common Core's background, which has roots that stretch more than a hundred years back. It is called Common Core today, but will soon be renamed, just as what happened with Progressive Education, Mastery Learning, Moral Relevancy/No Absolutes, Outcome Based Education, America 2000, Goals 2000, and No Child Left Behind. Common Core is the latest effort by a progressive, autocratic elite to completely *transfer all decisions* concerning children from parents, teachers and school boards to themselves, and to completely *transform America* from a nation of responsible, moral, independent human beings endowed by their Creator with unalienable rights of life, liberty and the pursuit of happiness to robots and servants of the state. These self-selected elites include big government businessmen, media, education think tanks, and labor organizations (Republicans and Democrats). (See Chapter Six for how this came about.)

I t will not be stopped until the decision-making is returned to those closest to the children. To return the decision-making for the education of our children means first understanding **who** the power brokers are, **how** they got the power, **what** they are implementing in the classroom, and what they **intend to do** with the power. How to reverse this process starts with knowledge, then understanding and wisdom, and then a plan. This book will focus on the important pieces of the puzzle and lay out a plan that, with enough Americans awakened, will enable us to take back the education of our children and in turn, America.

As President Reagan stated in 1961:

Freedom is never more than one generation away from extinction. We didn't pass it on to our children in the bloodstream. It must be fought for, protected, and handed on for them to do the same, or one day we will spend our sunset years telling our children and our children's children what it was once like in the United States where men were free.

CHAPTER 1

COMMON CORE & TRANSFORMATION

THE LONG WAR

*To change a free nation into a
captive nation of robots and zombies,
indoctrinate them with what to think
instead of teaching them how to think,
while removing all moral absolutes.*

1
COMMON CORE &
TRANSFORMATION

THE *LONG WAR*

JOHN DEWEY is reported to have said, **"You can't make Socialists out of individualists** – children who know how to think for themselves spoil the harmony of the collective society which is coming, where everyone is interdependent."[1] (Emphasis added.)

We are in a war ... not just a battle, and Common Core is the latest campaign that is the current front line of this war. It follows previous skirmishes in the 1930s over Progressive Education, the 1950s over Secular Humanist Education, and more recently in the 1990s over Outcome Based Education. All of these strategies are based on the premise of "progressive experts," instead of mom, dad and the teacher, setting common standards for all children. And since these secular, utopian standards drive the curriculum and assessments, local control of education ceases to be a reality.

On December 4, 2012, Bill Ayers (mentor to President Obama and today a high priest of teacher education) explained that schools and the classroom were where (revolutionary, communist) change must happen. Sitting at a table at New York University in a meeting titled "Change the Stakes," he tells his audience: "That [change] is our job, [and that] if we want change to come ... we have to discuss the ... schools ... [and] classrooms, ... our job is movement building. ...When there is movement [change] on the ground, s*** happens."[2]

In order to change a free nation into a captive nation, you need to control the minds of the next generation – through the schools and culture. Italian communist Antonio Gramsci called it *"the long march through culture;"* in other words, cultural Marxism sold through the schools, media, and culture ... *the long war*. This produces a generation hostile to freedom while rendering them unprotected against an enemy intent on conquering the free world with a ideology antagonistic to freedom.

It has become *the long war* to remake America.

The Origins of Common Core

From the Soviet-infiltrated Frankfurt School and Italian communist Antonio Gramsci, to social justice/Marxist William (Bill) Ayers, the plan was formed to turn America from freedom and liberty to a totalitarian oligarchy through the schools and culture. Adding further anti-Christian dimensions was evolutionist Charles Darwin and secular humanist/ socialist John Dewey and his cohorts at Columbia University Teacher's College, while Marxist Howard Zinn's, *A People's History of the United States*, helped destroy the memory of American exceptionalism and brought social justice (renamed, Marxism) into the classroom.

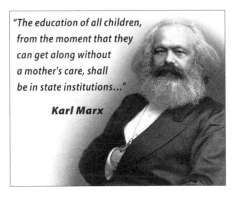

"The education of all children, from the moment that they can get along without a mother's care, shall be in state institutions..."

Karl Marx

These revolutionary educational movers, movements, and ideas coalesced in 1965, when President Lyndon Johnson created and passed, as a part of the "war on poverty," the *Elementary and Secondary Education Act* (ESEA). For the first time, education became an official federal program, even though it was not one of the legal areas for federal involvement specified in the Constitution. This law cleverly authorized federally-funded education programs, administered by the states, effectively shifting decision-making from the local to the federal. In 2002, Congress amended ESEA and reauthorized it as the *No Child Left Behind Act*. Social justice planners were delighted and went to work.

THE FRANKFURT SCHOOL: In his article titled, "The Frankfurt School and 'Political Correctness'," Michael Minnicino suggests that "the concept of the human soul was undermined by the most vociferous intellectual campaign ..."[3] It has brought us to the point that, "We will have to face the fact that the ugliness we see around us has been consciously fostered and organized in such a way, that **a majority of the population is losing the cognitive ability to transmit to the next generation, the ideas and methods upon which our civilization was built.** ..."[4] (Emphasis added.)

"The single, most important organizational component of this conspiracy was a Communist thinktank, called the Institute for Social Research (I.S.R.) [*Institut für Sozialforschung*], but popularly known as the Frankfurt School. ...[5]"

"Fleeing to the Soviet Union after the counter-revolution, [George] Lukacs [a Hungarian aristocrat] was secreted into Germany in 1922, where he chaired a meeting of Communist-oriented sociologists and intellectuals. This meeting founded the Institute for Social Research. Over the next decade, the Institute worked out what was to become the Comintern's[6] [Lenin and continuing with Stalin] most successful psychological warfare operation against the capitalist West.

"Lukacs identified that any political movement capable of bringing Bolshevism to the West would have to be, in his words, 'demonic'; it would have to 'possess the religious power which is capable of filling the entire soul; a power that characterized primitive Christianity'. However, Lukacs suggested, such a 'messianic' political movement could only succeed when the individual believes that his or her actions are determined by 'not a personal destiny, but the **destiny of the community**' in a world '*that has been abandoned by God* [emphasis added-MJM]'. [Emphasis added.]

"This abandonment of the soul's uniqueness also solves the problem of 'the diabolic forces lurking in all violence' which must be unleashed in order to create a revolution. ... once man has understood his alienation from God, then any act in the service of the 'destiny of the community' is justified; such an act can be 'neither crime nor madness. ... For crime and madness are objectifications of transcendental homelessness'. ...[7]

"The task of the Frankfurt School, then, was first, to undermine the Judeo-Christian legacy through an 'abolition of culture'..."[8] Lukacs, also developed the idea of "Revolution and Eros – sexual instinct used as an instrument of destruction."[9]

Many of the founders fled to United States university campuses in the 1930 and 1940s where their philosophy prevailed. Ralph de Toledano, co-founder of *National Review,* called the gathering of the Frankfurt School "perhaps more harmful to Western civilization than the Bolschevik Revolution itself."[10] His book, *Cry Havoc,* as reviewed by *Human Events,* says,

> "To a great extent, the conspiracy succeeded, and de Toledano recounts in brutal detail how the cluster of intellectuals around the Institute of Social Research became the powerful group known as the Frankfurt School. ... but the greatest harm came when the Frankfurt School decamped to America, courtesy of John Dewey and Columbia University. ... 'John Dewey's sponsorship gave the Institute a lock on Teacher's College – the foremost educational institution in the U.S. The influence of Teacher's College, in fact, reached out across the country, as its graduates filled more than 60 percent of all teaching and educational and administrative posts in the country'."[11]

ANTONIO GRAMSCI (1891-1937) was an Italian Marxist theoretician and politician who wrote on political theory, sociology and linguistics. He was a founding member and one-time leader of the Communist Party of Italy. In 1926, he was imprisoned by Benito Mussolini's Fascist regime. His theory of cultural hegemony, which describes how states use cultural institutions to maintain power in capitalist societies, was the bedrock of his "long war through the culture." It was based on the idea that the ruling class would manipulate the culture of that society — the beliefs, explanations, perceptions, values, and mores — so that their worldview is imposed and becomes accepted as the cultural norm. He has a large international following today and became the role model, along with the Frankfurt School transplants of socialist radicals in the United States, especially in the field of education and media/entertainment.

BILL AYERS was one of the communist/socialist radicals who tried to take over the United States through open revolution in the streets in the 1960s. Failing to turn the United States into a communist country by open revolution, Ayers redirected his energies and got his teaching degree, ultimately ending up as professor in the College of Education at the University of Illinois-Chicago, near the Chicago Laboratory Schools founded by John Dewey. From there, Ayers was heavily involved in educating future teachers and writing curriculum. During an interview with a college radio station on April 12, 2002, Ayers said, "I considered myself partly an anarchist then and

> **Ayers favors jettisoning chronological traditional Western civilization history and its accompanying classical literature.**

consider myself partly an anarchist now. I mean I'm as much an anarchist as I am a Marxist ... I'm very open about what I think."[12]

Ayers left his bomb building and throwing behind, in favor of training teachers and curriculum writing. In his book, *A Simple Justice, The Challenge of Small Schools*, as well as in his educational proposals, Ayers picks up the philosophy of (Marxist) Gramsci and the Frankfurt School. In the Foreword of *A Simple Justice*, he talks about "the quest for equality and social justice ... the imperatives of social change ... [and resisting] the blinding mystifying power of the familiar social evils – racism, sexism and homophobia. ... Education is contested space ... over questions of justice."[13] In Chapter 1, Ayers complains about teachers who have "an unhealthy obsession with classroom management and linear lesson plans. ... [And rhetorically asks] How does authoritative knowledge deny some kids' experiences?"[14]

The Ayers – Gramsci Connection

In other words, Ayers favors jettisoning chronological traditional Western civilization history and its accompanying classical literature. According to *American Thinker's* Linda Kimball, Gramsci taught that,

"... [The] Christianized West was the obstacle standing in the way of a communist new world order. The West would have to be conquered first.

"Gramsci posited that because Christianity had been dominant in the West for over 2000 years, not only was it fused with Western civilization, but it had corrupted the worker class. The West would have to be de-Christianized, said Gramsci, by means of a *'long march through the culture.'* Additionally, a new proletariat must be created. ... The new battleground, reasoned Gramsci, must become the culture, starting with the traditional family and completely engulfing churches, schools, media, entertainment, civic organizations, literature, science, and history. All of these things must be radically transformed and the social and cultural order gradually turned upside-down with the new proletariat placed in power at the top."[15] Gramsci's philosophy melded with that of the Frankfurt School: *Destroy the moral foundations of America.*

HOWARD ZINN, who "described himself as 'something of an anarchist, something of a socialist, maybe a democratic socialist',"[16] wrote the lead endorsement on the back cover of Ayer's *A Simple Justice.* Zinn's wildly popular history textbook is classic social justice/victimization with the United States as **the villain.** "He wrote … *A People's History of the United States,* to provide other perspectives on American history. The textbook depicts the struggles of Native Americans against European and U.S. conquest and expansion, slaves against slavery, unionists and other workers against capitalists, women against patriarchy, and African-Americans for civil rights."[17] Zinn's contempt for the West is displayed in his textbooks where he maintains that "American history is nothing to be proud of; on the contrary, it is nothing more than one long, disgraceful record of oppression, genocide and exploitation."[18] Insight into Zinn's teachings is expounded well in the 2014 DVD, *America, Imagine a World Without Her,* by Dinesh D'Souza.

Enter Big Business and Governors

Building upon the *long march through culture* of Gramsci, Dewey and Ayers, a group of big businessmen, governors, and top national and state educators joined together to "solve the education problem" and institute workforce education. By 2009, the National Governors Association (NGA) and the Council of Chief State School Officers (CCSSO), along with and through their proxy organization, Achieve, had formed the Common Core State Standards Initiative to develop a set of standards for **all** the states, which they copyrighted privately. Contrary to the official statements, the **states did not** write them. Working hand in glove with these organizations using 2009 stimulus money, the Federal Department of Education offered a pot of money in a competition called "Race to the Top." The enticement to join was,"*Sign a blank contract and you may win the money.*" Almost all the states signed contracts to adopt standards *not yet written.* **Few won the money**. Today, enabling them are Bill Gates' millions supporting Common Core proponents and especially helping fund the public relations for Common Core.

Much of what happened in the 1990s in education set the stage for how the National Governors Association, educators and businessmen shifted local control of education to federal control. The organization, Achieve, became its face, and its underlying progressive/social justice mission was further validated when Bill Ayers was the lunchtime keynote speaker at the Renaissance

Group's 20th Anniversary Celebration in Washington, D.C. (October 4-6, 2009). The Renaissance Group is a national consortium working to prepare American education professionals. It was at this meeting that Achieve's president, Nevin Brown (along with Secretary of Education Duncan and other notables), launched to the world the Common Core Standards Initiative.[20]

What IS Common Core?

Ultimately, Common Core becomes a **national curriculum** *enforced* by national assessments and *controlled* by anti-western elites through an immense and deeply *invasive* collection of individual data. The cost? Apart from the loss of freedom, it is astronomical. Consider the price tag of the mandate that every child in America will have to have access to a computer to receive curriculum and take assessments. Then add in the need to update the computers every few years (Microsoft and Bill Gates) and the bureaucrats needed to develop and maintain this monstrosity. Contrary to its claims, Common Core:

~ ~ ~

Since 1996, Achieve has been running the show, and from its own website it gives us a time line. Among their claims:

• "Achieve is proud to be the leading voice for the college- and career-ready agenda, and has helped transform the concept of 'college and career readiness for all students' from a radical proposal into a national agenda. … and helps…to prepare all young people for postsecondary education, work, and citizenship. …

• Work begins on the development of the Common Core State Standards; Achieve partners with the National Governors Association and Council of Chief State School Officers on the Initiative, and a number of Achieve staff and consultants serve on the writing and review teams. (2009)

• The final Common Core State Standards are released; Achieve begins serving as Project Management Partner for the Partnership for Assessment of Readiness for College and Careers (PARCC). (2010) [PARCC is one of the two federally supported primary assessment groups tasked with implementing Common Core.]

• Achieve begins managing the state-led development of the K-12 Next Generation Science Standards." (2011)[19]

- is **not** state-led and controlled (the feds dictate the terms);
- is **not** voluntary (states will lose federal money if not in compliance);
- **will** drive curriculum where schools will teach to the federal tests; and
- **is** funded and enforced by the federal government and its crony elites.

Mission, Philosophy & Worldview of Common Core

Because Common Core ultimately becomes thought control, the mission, philosophy and worldview of those behind it must be further examined. An in-depth examination of the curriculum from the past forty years as well as the Common Core Standards, reveals *fractured thinking* immersed in socialism/social justice. *The rich complexities and ambiguities of human life have been reduced to simple formulas about oppressors and the oppressed, capitalists and workers, Western imperialist and their non-Western victims.* The way social justice works is that third party elites pick whom to favor with government largess, while taking the money needed to fund their schemes through the strong arm of taxes and regulation. The *classical* education of seeking truth in an *orderly* way with *chronologically* historic facts including *sequential* mathematic exercises has been replaced. Fractured thinking and a smorgasbord of short snippets of literature and history without context, mathematics without logic, and science based on a *political* agenda instead of the *scientific* method are now the standard.

Destroying National Values

With teachers educated by the revolutionaries and using revolutionary curriculum, American education has produced a divided America consisting of the oppressed and the oppressors. The philosophy of victimology is reflected in U.S. history where the Howard Zinns and others have concentrated on group identity and power struggles instead of individual liberty and opportunity. Instead of the public schools being the melting pot of America and immigrants striving to become Americans, today they divide into race, sex, and gender until all, not just immigrants, become hyphenated Americans.

In *The Victims' Revolution, The Rise of Identity Studies and the Closing of the Liberal Mind*, author Bruce Bawer's Preface notes that "Americans lament the loss of shared national values,"[21] but do not understand that it is more than that, it is a "rejection, indeed the demonization, of the very ideas that once defined" America. He quotes "celebrated liberal historian" Arthur Schlesinger, Jr., pointing out that "what holds a nation together" for two

> **America was built on a brand-new national identity by individuals who, in forsaking old loyalties and joining to make new lives, melted away ethnic differences.**

hundred years has been replaced with a "brand-new **national identity** by individuals who, in forsaking old loyalties and joining to make new lives, melted away ethnic differences."[22] (Emphasis added.) Bawer observes, "To point out the miraculous nature of their accomplishment [America's cohesiveness] – its utter lack of precedent in all of human history ... is to note that, in a world where violent intergroup enmity and conflict have been the rule rather than the exception, America found a way for increasingly diverse groups of people to live together not only in peace but with a strong sense of **shared identity** – an identity founded not on ethnicity, but on commitment to the values of individual liberty, dignity, and equality articulated in the Declaration of Independence and the Constitution"[23] and we would add, in Judeo-Christian foundations.

Multiculturalism

Bawer notes that Schlesinger lamented "the most disastrous by-product of the civil rights movement was multiculturalism, a philosophy that teaches, as Schlesinger put it, 'that America is not a nation of individuals at all but a nation of groups.' For two centuries, Americans had been held together by a shared sense of **national identity**, a belief in individual liberty, and a vision of full equality ... [but] the very idea of a shared identity began to be challenged, condemned, dismantled – and replaced with a new conception, founded not on individual rights and liberties, but on the claims of group identity and culture."[24] **National identity** is codified in the Declaration of Independence and the United States Constitution and is underscored by the biblical worldview.

The Socialist/Marxist/social justice crowd has successfully forced classrooms to sort everything by **groups** of victims and has even succeeded in creating an America where civil discussions between friends have been reduced to anger and hostility over perceived victims. Anger, and even hatred, reign over Christian love and compassion. Group thinking has even impacted assessments with group answers instead of individual answers; *individual accountability is lost as is individual identity.* An in-depth study of the Frankfurt School goals reveals their success at "[unleashing] the diabolic forces lurking in all violence ... in order to create a revolution."[25]

A reflection of how successful the message has been is evident in the recent and ongoing demonstrations coming out of the August 9, 2014, shooting in Ferguson, Missouri. The lack of moral responsibility and "diabolic forces lurking in all violence" was obvious as a teen was seen on camera bullying and robbing a recently immigrated shop owner.

Individual responsibility has given way to group entitlement, as America is being divided and conquered by the Marxists of the Frankfurt School and their agenda.

CHAPTER 2

CHANGING THE PURPOSE OF EDUCATION

SABOTAGING THE SOUL

*Common Core is ultimately the
struggle for the soul of America.*

2
CHANGING THE PURPOSE
OF EDUCATION

SABOTAGING THE SOUL

THOUGH THE BATTLE for the brains of American children is real, it is equally a battle for their souls. ***Common Core is ultimately the struggle for the soul of America***. And, unless America collectively endorses education as the search for truth, all matters philosophical, religious, and eternal cease to exist in the educational institutions.

The Changing Face of Our World
SUSIE'S STORY

*She didn't **want to**, she tried **not to,** she "tried to be brave," her friends cried and one even tried to call home, but in the end ... she **had to**.*[1]

On Tuesday March 19, 1996, she **had to**, as did 58 other sixth-graders at the J. T. Lambert Intermediate School in East Stroudsburg, Pennsylvania. Susie Tucker and the other "girls were ... individually called into the doctor's [nurse's] office. This was not a normal school nurse visit, because "they were required to remove their underwear, lay on the table and spread their legs for the exam."[2] It included "an examination of genitals."[3] Some of the girls "asked not to have their genitals examined, but were told they **had to**."[4] (Emphasis added.) Later, "some parents told school officials that their daughters were given an internal gynecological exam ... [but] the East Stroudsburg pediatrician who performed the exams, [said] there was only an external examination of genitalia with some touching, which is within parameters set by the State Department of Health."[5]

Susie Tucker "broke down ... while describing the fear many girls felt while waiting half-clothed for the exam."[6] Later, she wrote, "I don't have hysteria ... I want justice, I want to stop the insomnia, the waking up at 2 a.m. and not being able to get back to sleep, I want to stop the nightmares, the feeling of being violated, I want to get my power back ..."[7]

AMERICA'S STORY

How does this tie into what has happened in America's streets that are no longer safe? Or where our children must be subjected to humiliating and frightening physical exams and frisked or forced to pass through metal detectors before they enter school? What has happened to cause our senior citizens to fear venturing out at night or to cower in their own homes out of terror that someone may break in and rob them? When we look for answers, we blithely accept leaders who lie, cheat and "feel our pain." Yet, we reject leaders who tell us things that make us "uncomfortable." Perhaps answers can be found starting with an event that took place over 90 years ago.

THE STAGE IS SET. The day was July 10, 1925, the location Tennessee, and the event, an amazing trial that was just concluding. The main player was a science teacher named John Thomas Scopes. As the *Encyclopedia Britannica* reports, "it seems to have been rather the trial of a religious movement, Fundamentalism, than that of an individual."

"Scopes, a teacher of science in Rhea High School, (sic) Dayton, was arrested on a charge of violating the Tennessee state law prohibiting the teaching in public schools of any theories that deny the divine creation of man as taught in the Bible. Scopes, a biologist, had been teaching evolution. The immediate issue was as to whether the defendant had or had not violated the provisions of the state law as to the subjects to be taught in public schools, but the wider issue was as to the extent to which the state, in its control of public education, may determine the nature of the religious instruction given to the students in its schools. The trial itself was the culmination of a controversy that had been going on for years.

"William Jennings Bryan, a firm believer in the literal interpretation of the Bible, went to Dayton to assist the prosecution. Widespread popular interest was manifested in the case, which in the hands of Bryan, and Clarence Darrow and Dudley Field Malone, defense counsels, assumed the form of a contest between fundamentalism and modernism.

"The outcome was that on July 21, Scopes was found guilty and fined $100, but the penalty was set aside by the state supreme court on a technicality, without any expression of opinion as to the constitutionality of the law. Bryan had been prevented, through the tactics of Darrow from delivering the elaborate speech which he had prepared in refutation of Darwin's theories."[8]

Although it was otherwise, history textbooks would have us believe that Scopes was innocent. Why? In the ensuing years, Darwin's Theory of Evolution came to be taught in the schools, and Fundamentalism or Creationism was forbidden. Somehow, the winner became the loser, and the loser became the winner. Also lost was the understanding that God created man, which then gave way to the idea of an evolved man with no purpose or unique value. The Scopes trial helped to open the door further to the Frankfurt School's goal of undermining the Judeo-Christian legacy.

THE ORIGIN OF MAN – *SLIME vs. SCRIPTURE*

Who is man? Is he, as evolutionists claim, nothing more than a blob of slime that has evolved into a more complex animal **or** just a human resource, as labeled by education and the government, placing man in the same material resource category as plants, animals and manufactured goods where resource implies something to be used by society?[9]

With the change of the basic concept from creation to evolution, man's total purpose on earth becomes to *be of use to society.* Society then determines what his function is, what happens when he ceases to be useful and whether he possesses a value other than what society has assigned.

If man "evolved," as evolutionists teach, then what is the basis for man's value? Nothing in evolution suggests that man possesses an innate value or that it is possible for his value to be entirely different from plants and animals. There must be a power outside of man to give him that value.

If evolution is the explanation for man's existence, then it stands to reason that the society in which he exists determines his value. If society determines his value, it must also set limits on that value and control it. How does society control man's value? It controls that value by force or by whomever has the power to carry out that force. What then does society do about someone like Hitler who acquired that force and defined the value of man his own way?

PRE-SCOPES AMERICA

For three hundred years, pre-Scopes Christian America believed that man was created in the image of God. If man is created in the image of God, then he has value given to him by his Creator, **not by men**. He is valuable not because society says so, but rather because of his innate being, a being created in the image of the Creator. Pre-Scopes America based its laws and values on biblical Judeo-Christian teachings. Its schools, churches and synagogues taught that each person was precious in the sight of God. Every person was to be treated with respect and dignity because man's image was God's image, and God Himself was to be respected and treated with dignity. One of the first and most widely used books to teach Americans in the 1600s and 1700s was the *New England Primer*, which teaches the alphabet with biblical illustrations such as, "A – In Adam's fall, we sinned all."[10] The 1900 edition described the impact of the *Primer*:

> "The *New England Primer* was one of the greatest books ever published. It went through innumerable editions; it reflected in a marvelous way the spirit of the age that produced it, and contributed perhaps more than any other book except the *Bible*, to the molding of those sturdy generations that gave to America its liberty and its institutions."[11]

In the mid to late 1800s and early 1900s, the textbook series most widely used was *McGuffy's Readers* which includes in its Primer:

> "Do you see that tall tree? Long ago it sprang up from a small nut.

> "It was God, my child. God made the world and all things in it. He made the sun to light the day, and the moon to shine at night. God shows that he loves us by all that he has done for us. Should we not then love him?"[12]

Americans understood, prior to Scopes, that man was a product of a divine Creator, had "fallen," and was capable of evil. Until he was redeemed by a Savior, as both the Jewish and Christian sacred writings taught, he would not be free from evil. Did that make America full of crime, distress and anger? No, the teaching inherent in the "Fundamentalism" of William

Jennings Bryan was that man was "fallen" and "sinful," and because of that, man would always struggle with evil while on earth. This belief lent strength to the public schools, reinforcing the Judeo-Christian teachings of the family, teaching that the child needed constant reminders of who God was, what the Old and New Testament taught about right and wrong, and why the child needed to pattern his behavior after biblical virtues.

The need of society, through its families, churches and schools, was to civilize the child. Webster's 1828 Dictionary defines "civilize" as "to reclaim from a savage state; to introduce civility of manners among a people and instruct them in the arts of regular life."[13] In pre-Scopes America, "to civilize" meant teaching the Old and New Testament as the basis of society. Post-Scopes, it has come to mean that since man is no different than slime, plants or animals, and because he is not responsible to any higher authority, he is now free to "do his own thing."

Noah Webster (1758-1843), author of the 1828 Dictionary, noted:

> "It is extremely important to our nation, in a political as well as religious view that all possible authority and influence should be given to the Scriptures, for these furnish the best principles of liberty, and the most effectual support of republican government. The principles of all genuine liberty, and wise laws and administrations are to be drawn from the Bible and sustained by its authority. The man therefore who weakens or destroys the divine authority of that book may be accessory to all the public disorders which society is doomed to suffer."[14]

We are facing "public disorders" as Noah Webster noted. Ask any senior citizen or inner city youth if there could there be a correlation between what we have been teaching and the behavior of our present-day society. Has our society "turned humans into animals"? Has the street become "a jungle"? Is the mob mentality of violence and entitlement in today's cities an example of the latest manifestation?

FROM CLASSROOM TO LIFE

If we teach our young people that they originated from apes, it is no wonder that they act like apes. When a society teaches its young that there is no higher authority than themselves, they cannot be expected to respect an authority that punishes what it arbitrarily defines as bad. When children are taught that good and bad are relative terms or values, we should expect dichotomies to arise where good becomes bad and bad becomes good. Can society then enforce codes that punish those who have been taught to view everything as relative, unless those who hold the most power in society arbitrarily dictate when and if a law has been broken? When a society deems that man has *no* intrinsic value, it treats him however those in power determine he is to be treated. Ultimately, the view by education and government that man is a only a resource (or matter, as evolutionary experts would have us believe) makes him expendable, discardable, and destined to eventually become worthless when it is determined that he no longer has value.

AMERICA'S FOUNDING DOCUMENTS

PRE-SCOPES AMERICA understood the content incorporated in the *Declaration of Independence* when it said:

> *"We hold these Truths to be self-evident, that all Men are created equal, that they are endowed by their Creator with certain unalienable Rights, that among these are Life, Liberty, and the Pursuit of Happiness – That to secure these Rights, Governments are instituted among Men, deriving their just Powers from the Consent of the Governed ..."*

Clearly, the Declaration stated that man **was** created by a divine Creator and that he did not evolve. It also reinforced the understanding that man was given his existence, freedom and choice of vocation by God, not the government. This was one of the original foundation stones of pre-Scopes America. In no way would the founders have ever thought of man as a descendant of apes. Man was *not* a resource existing for the pleasure of society, but rather he was given resources by God in order to pursue his own dreams and plans and add to society.

A study of the writings of America's founders, as well as the United States Constitution, attests to the understanding that man could not be accountable just to man, but had to be accountable to a greater power: a Creator God. The balance of powers (checks and balances and the federal system) are good illustrations of how the founders did not trust man with concentrated and unlimited power. In fact, "The framers of our Constitution believed firmly with Montesquieu [a French magistrate, and author in 1748 of *Spirit of Laws*] that: 'When the legislative and executive powers are united in the same person, or in the same body of magistrates, there can be no liberty ...' "[15]

Clearly, a society's definition of **who** man is and where he comes from makes a difference in what its people value and helps determine its foundation stones. Once America began viewing man as matter or as a resource alone, we were on the path for the next "reformer" to lay a new kind of building stone for the emerging *Great Community* or what became known as the *Village*.

HOW DID EDUCATION BECOME OUR SAVIOR?

The evaporation of religious faith among the educated left a vacuum in the minds of Western intellectuals easily filled by secular superstition.[16] Paul Johnson

As the ramifications of the Scopes trial began to seep into the fabric of America, other factors were being woven into the picture. Dramatic economic and social changes occurred in the country in the 1920s and 1930s. On a broader scale, noted historian Paul Johnson describes Europe following World War I:

"The old order had gone ... A new order would eventually take its place ... disquieting currents of thought ... [suggested] the image of the world adrift, having left its moorings in traditional law and morality ... Marx described a world in which the central dynamic was economic interest. To Freud, the principal thrust was sexual. Both assumed that religion, the old impulse that moved men and masses, was a fantasy and always had been ... the decline and ultimately the collapse of the religious impulse would leave a huge vacuum ... In place of religious belief, there would be a secular ideology. Those who had once filled the ranks of the totalitarian clergy would become totalitarian politicians. And, above all, the Will to Power would produce a new kind of messiah, uninhibited by any religious sanctions whatever, and with an unappeasable appetite for controlling mankind. The end of the old order, with an unguided world adrift in a relativistic universe, was a summons to such gangster-statesmen to emerge. They were not slow to make their appearance."[17]

America's Blind Trust

America was not far behind. The new savior/messiah became education. As Paul Johnson notes:

"Between 1910 and 1930 total educational spending rose fourfold, from $426.25 million to $2.3 billion; higher education spending increased fourfold too, to nearly one billion a year. Illiteracy fell during the period from 7.7 to 4.3 percent ... more new books were bought than ever before but there was a persistent devotion to the classics."[18]

Meanwhile, America's middle class came into its own, and affluence, not just subsistence, became a way of life for many. Admonitions against "that devil drink" fell upon deaf ears as the growing middle class ignored the prohibition against alcohol. They grew accustomed to disobeying the law in the pursuit of pleasure. Never mind that the law was misguided in its attempt to legislate morality. Many Christians deserted their churches as the religious institutions embraced liberalism's abandonment of the inerrancy of Scripture, and those left in churches became embroiled in destructive schisms.

A temporary check was put on the growing free-spiritedness when the stock market crashed in 1929, ushering in the Great Depression. In spite of the fact that one in four men were unemployed in the 1930s, there was little crime. Times of adversity forced Americans to come together as families and help each other. Priorities became simple: enough food, a roof over your head, a job, and a supportive family. The wild days of prohibition followed by the stock market crash had momentarily sobered Americans. But not for long.

Modern Ideas

With the advent of World War II, America's industry once again began to hum with jobs, putting most men back to work. Americans paid little attention to what was happening in education. Schools still responded to parents and were teaching the three "R's" (reading, 'riting and 'rithmetic). However, largely unknown was the impact that the social justice revolutionaries and Charles Darwin were having on the teachers' colleges and, in turn, the new incoming teachers. Gradually, *revolutionary* ideas began to take hold. Schools started abandoning the age-old and tested method of teaching reading phonetically, for the newer model of *look-say*. Children lost their love of reading, because they struggled to memorize words versus being able to decode them. *Progressive* education began spreading during the war years from experimental schools to small towns and big cities as new teachers brought new *progressive* educational methods learned in the universities, and with them, hastened the reading problems of modern education.

But additional changes were occurring in the realm of politics. As Paul Johnson puts it,

"The big change in principle came under [John F.] Kennedy. ... Kennedy introduced a new concept of 'big government,' the 'problem eliminator': ... Every area of human misery could be classified as a 'problem'; then the Federal government could be armed to 'eliminate' it ...

[Kennedy's successor, Lyndon B. Johnson started the legislative process.] "The bills came rolling out: the Elementary and Secondary Education Act, the Medicare Act ...

"It was an old liberal belief ... that universal education alone could make democracy tolerable ... In the 1950s the myth that education was the miracle cure for society emerged stronger than ever. No one believed in it more devotedly than [Lyndon] Johnson. As President, he said: **'The answer for all our national problems comes in a single word. The word is education.'**...

"It was confidently expected that this vast investment in human resources would not only stimulate growth still further but achieve moral and social purposes ..."[19]

The net result was that huge amounts of money began to flow to the educational establishments, particularly to the universities where the researchers, with their laboratories, resided. As the professors and researchers turned out their papers, textbook companies picked up on the trends. In a very short time, most of the textbooks, reflecting the priorities of the Frankfurt School, included the concepts of relativism, values clarification and self-actualization. When School To Work developed, workforce and career education became the buzz words.

Dewey Follows Darwin

Add to this the growing influence of John Dewey (1859-1952), considered the leading educational philosopher in America in the twentieth century. Dewey, born the year Darwin published *On the Origin of Species*, became an early follower of Darwin and his theory of evolution. In an address prepared for Kappa Delta Pi at Columbia University in 1909, Dewey said,

"In laying hands upon the sacred ark of absolute permanency, in treating the forms that had been treated as the types of fixity and perfection as originating and passed away, the *Origin of Species* introduced a mode of thinking that in the end was bound to transform the logic of knowledge, and hence the treatment of morals, politics, and religion."[20]

What exactly did Dewey believe education should be? The editor of the Kappa Delta Pi lecture series sums up Dewey as proposing "the 'new' school ... should *no longer* 'prepare the young for future responsibilities and for success in life, by means of acquisition of the organized bodies of information and prepared forms of skill which comprehend the material of instruction.' ..."[21] He opposed "Imposition from above; ... external discipline; ... learning from texts and teachers; ... acquisition of isolated skills and techniques by drill; ... preparation for a more or less remote future; ... [and] static aims and materials."[22] In other words, Dewey opposed building a knowledge base.

Right and Wrong

Dewey's emphasis on experience as opposed to intellectual acquisition became his trademark. In the book, *Experience and Education,* he struggled with the idea of good and bad experiences

Dewey claimed: There is no God, and there is no soul.

and never came to a conclusion. While he was promoting experience over traditional knowledge acquisition, he was involved in the writing of the 1933 *Humanist Manifesto.* His idea of right and wrong is reflected in the *Manifesto.* In *A Common Faith*, Dewey stated, "Here [in the *Manifesto*] are all the elements for a religious faith that shall not be confined to sect, class or race ... It remains to make it explicit and militant."[23] The *Manifesto* describes the world as "self existing and not created." Dewey himself said that "Geological discoveries have displaced Creation myths ... [and] Biology [has] revolutionized conceptions of soul and mind which once occupied a central place in religious beliefs and ideas."[24] He further said that "There is no God and there is no soul. Hence, there are no needs for the props of traditional religion. With dogma and creed excluded, then immutable truth is also dead and buried. There is no room for fixed, natural law – or moral absolutes."[25]

Authority and Absolutes

So, when Dewey says, "When external authority is rejected, it does not follow that all authority should be rejected, but rather that there is need to search for a more effective source of authority,"[26] we must ask what or who becomes that authority. Since Dewey rejects moral absolutes, and evolution has thrown out an external, divine God, then man himself becomes the source of authority. Is it then reasonable to suggest that he who has the control and the power *is* the authority? With Dewey's emphasis on experience as the ultimate in education, and his rejection of moral absolutes, the stage is set for education and schools to focus on *experience not governed by moral absolutes.*

Although Dewey said as early as 1929 that he "thought the problem was not how to prolong prosperity (he took that for granted) but how to turn the 'Great Society' into the 'Great Community.' "[27] It was not until the 1940s that we get a picture of what that *Great Community,* or the *Village,* would look like.

THE NEW GOD – SEX

The Kinsey Report

It was the publication of Dr. Alfred Kinsey's studies of the sexual behavior of human males (1948) and human females (1953) that "more than any other document in history ... shaped Western society's beliefs and understanding about human sexuality ... Their impact on attitudes, subsequent developments in sexual behavior, politics, law, sex education and even religion has been immense ..."[28] These documents were the conclusions of Kinsey's "scientific" investigations of human sexual behaviors in the 1940s and 1950s.

"The results of the Kinsey surveys on sexual behavior of the American male and female *established, to some degree, social standards of what was acceptable common practice.*"[29] Although as his associate Wardell Pomeroy pointed out, Kinsey "was the most talked about and least read author of our time; the majority of people got their opinions of his work second hand."[30]

SIECUS Sets Up Shop

The Kinsey Report enabled sex education in the classroom. The Sex Information and Education Council of the United States. (SIECUS) was established in 1964. Taking the initiative, it described itself as "the *only* organization in the United States that acts as an advocate for human sexuality and provides information and education in sexual matters through a clearing house and resource center."[31] The initial grant for the Office of Research Services of SIECUS was made early in the 1960s by the Playboy Foundation.[32] Very quickly, it became the instigator and provider of materials for the teaching of sex education in the schools. In 1982 Mary Calderone, a co-founder of SIECUS, described the relationship between SIECUS and Kinsey,

"The great library collection of what is now known as the Kinsey Institute in Bloomington, Indiana, was formed ... with one major field omitted: sex education. This was because it seemed appropriate ... to its major funding source, the National Institute of Mental Health, [a U.S. government agency] to leave this area for SIECUS to fill ... [SIECUS was] approved for a highly important grant from the National Institute for Mental Health that was designed ... for SIECUS to become the primary data base for the area of education for sexuality."[33]

Sex Education Textbooks

With Kinsey, *Playboy Magazine* and SIECUS all pushing sex education, the curricula used in American schools reveals the anti-family agenda. Starting in the late 1970s, *Person to Person,* a popular sex education school health text gave students a chance to "report to the others [in the class] your new definition of a family."[34] This is after the student has been introduced to a "communal group of four men and four women" and an "unmarried couple, male and female."[35] Later in the text, the student is given convincing arguments for "group marriages [good for lonely old folks where women outnumber men],[36] "and open marriages [that] allows spouses to develop their own interests ... people free to act in ways that will bring personal growth,"[37] and is told that "in traditional marriage, partners are expected to meet each other's needs ... marriage may come to seem like a cage."[38] Finally, the student is told to "express what you *feel* marriage is or should be."[39] (Emphasis added.) Note that there are no absolutes, and the ultimate answer is based on feelings, not knowledge. All this is in line with the goals of the Frankfurt School.

> **Classroom texts maintain that there are no absolutes. The ultimate answer is based on feelings, not knowledge.**

Literally thousands of examples of American sex education school materials could be cited, all of which promote these ideas: "no moral absolutes"; "feelings as the basis for decisions;" "promotion of sexual permissiveness" (as long as *protection* is used); and "abortion as an alternative to unwanted pregnancies."

When the Common Core exemplars came along in 2010 and included in their recommended literature, writings that numerous parents called pornographic, the ground had already been softened in the latter part of the twentieth century through sex education and such books used in the grade schools as Judy Blume's, *Then Again, Maybe I Won't* and Shel Silverstein's, *A Light in the Attic.* Blume's book was a young adult novel intended for pre-teens and teenagers that dealt with puberty from a male perspective as well as the other trials of growing up. Another Blume novel about a girl entering puberty and making the transition to womanhood was considered by many parents as offensive because of her inclusion of sexual language. Unknown to most parents, Shel Silverstein was the lead illustrator for *Playboy Magazine* with many of his drawings, as well as text, in his children's books reflective of the *Playboy* philosophy.

Values Clarification

> *Truth is the secret of eloquence and of virtue, the basis of moral authority; it is the highest summit of art and of life.* [40]
> Henri-Frederic Amiel

HASTENING THE DEMISE of a strong nuclear family based on absolutes of right and wrong and the sexualization of all students was the values clarification movement.

Values Clarification, a 1972 textbook, says,

"Bombarded by all these influences, the young person is ultimately left to make his own choice about whose advice or values to follow. But young people brought up by moralizing adults are not prepared to make their own responsible choices. They have not learned a process of selecting the best and rejecting the worst ... [Notice the terminology that it is *best*, not right and *worst*, not wrong.]

"The values-clarification approach tries to help young people ... build their own value system ... It is based on the approach formulated by Louis Raths, who in turn built upon the thinking of John Dewey ...

"Thus, the values-clarification approach does not aim to instill any particular set of values ..."[41]

With this widely used textbook, all truth became relative. If, as they said, goodness was inside each person, then each person was his own arbitrator of truth and goodness. The utopian society was under way. From the pens and laboratories of the self-actualizers and the values-clarifiers came a plethora of textbooks and classroom materials. Such things as "encounter groups," which became the popular thing to do in the 1960s and 1970s, led young people in high schools and college campuses across the nation to "get in touch with themselves" and "look to their inner selves for what was right or wrong." The end result in today's classrooms is for the students to "do their own thing."

> **The 1960s became the decade of riots and revolution; the 1970s brought sexual permissiveness and feel-good based decisions; and the 2000s led to the behavior of entitlement and moral relativity.**

Is it any wonder that the 1960s became the decade of riots and revolution on the campuses? Is it any wonder that in the 1970s sexual permissiveness, self-centeredness and "feel-good" based decisions opened the door for *relativism*? In Allan Bloom's 1987 best-seller, *The Closing of the American Mind*, he states, "There is one thing a professor can be absolutely certain of: Almost every student entering the university believes, or says he believes, that truth is relative."[42] Should anyone be surprised that in 2015, this behavior of entitlement and moral relativity was on exhibit as anarchists and revolutionaries marched in the streets of America protesting "police brutality" when young criminals were confronted?

ALDOUS HUXLEY states that a perfect totalitarian state is one where "they love their servitude."[43] Has anyone wondered how to make people *love servitude*? Wouldn't you first have to remove the questioning nature in people? If their focus becomes pleasure as the Frankfurt School promoted, and their material needs were always met, wouldn't this be a start? Then, wouldn't you keep them busy with jobs where they felt good about themselves? This was evident when news sources reported that American students scored low on math, but still had high self-esteem. They were confident about their math abilities, but did poorly on the test.[44]

Destroying the Culture

Evolution that designated man as a resource and not a creation of God laid the base of destruction. *Sex education* that focuses attention on satisfying one's pleasures and on unlimited, unrestrained sex that consumes time, purpose and resources contributed as did *relativism* that teaches children that there are no rights or wrongs.

Self-gratification interrupts the child's developmental cycle and prevents him from learning compassion, while presenting all learning by "feeling" and "touching" crushes the base of the culture (the Judeo-Christian worldview), making it "second class," obsolete and something to be "whispered" in the shadows. Finally, claiming that the *state* can solve all problems, replacing those private institutions that previously had addressed them, enslaves the individual to it.

The State is King

At the 1997 Philadelphia *In the Name of Youths Summit*,[45] President Bill Clinton said that America would "redefine the meaning of citizenship in America," and wanted Americans to be called "citizen-servants."[46] This follows the subtle shift in terminology in America from the *Declaration of Independence*, which said "Governments are instituted among Men, deriving their just Powers from the Consent of the Governed." The purpose of government becomes usurping the rights of the individual by turning him into a servant of the state instead of protecting his God-given individual rights, e.g., government as a servant. In the *Declaration*, there exists a hierarchy: God, the Creator, is at the top with the individual receiving his rights from God and then, by consent, delegating to the state some of those rights for things that the individual cannot do for himself. The Philadelphia Summit based its emotional appeal on America's capacity for charity and helping the down and out. However, that appeal stems from the *Village* concept whose building stones claim that the *state* is the primary source of all that is good in society and that each individual has a debt to society for that good. In other words, the *state* is the final arbitrator of the goodness of society.

SUSIE'S ORDEAL

Coming full circle, the *elites* at the Philadelphia Summit called for access to healthcare. Susie Tucker experienced the government's version of that health care.

"Genital exams needed, doctors tell school board," proclaimed the March 28, 1996, headline of the *Pocono Record*. After Dr. Ramleh Vahanvaty was accused of "inappropriately examining" the girls, eight area doctors sent a letter of support to the East Stroudsburg school board. They justified the exam. "Often, we find some (girls) with physical deformities which may get worse with sports activities, and others with contagious conditions (warts or vaginal lesions) that require immediate medical treatment."[47] Is it the state's function to insure that maturing girls' bodies are free from defect? Or is it the parents' function? The American Academy of Pediatrics' *School Health:*

A Guide for Health Professionals, 1987 revision, concludes, "while genital examination 'is usually *omitted* in school screening exams' it is an important part of the physical."[48] (Emphasis added.)

Susie Tucker tried to avoid such an invasive action, but to no avail. Her parents had not given permission, but that didn't matter to the school authorities. Allegedly, notes were sent home about the exam as well as permission slips to take the exam in school. However, according to one of the parents, "The school was unable to present any proof that parents ever received such notices."[49]

Perhaps this fixation on girl's sexuality comes from the Frankfurt School's most known proponent, Herbert Marcuse, who wrote "Eros and Civilization." Marcuse "promised that the overcoming of capitalism and its false consciousness will result in a society where the greatest satisfactions are sexual."[50] Today's implementation of ObamaCare locks this kind of abuse into place.

> *Our leaders must remember that education doesn't begin with some isolate bureaucrat in Washington. It doesn't even begin with state or local officials. Education begins in the home.*
>
> President Ronald Reagan

CHAPTER 3

THE STANDARDS

COMMON CORE INDOCTRINATION

Common Core sets into concrete the fractured thinking and progressive education of the past fifty years.

3
THE STANDARDS

COMMON CORE INDOCTRINATION

"Great is truth, but still greater from a practical point of view is silence about truth."[1] Aldous Huxley

PARENTS ARE LASHING out against Common Core by posting cell phone pictures on the *Internet* of their children struggling with homework. Children are crying out in anguish, because bad curriculum and faulty or sluggish computers place unrealistic and far-reaching demands on them.

Actual homework and textbook examples, as well as the examples given by the official Common Core copyrighted materials, are now available and clearly document the concerns of parents. Additionally, there exists a decidedly progressive, big-government, morally-equivalent worldview in much of the standards and assessments in literature, history, and science. Math is still *fuzzy*. Granted, much of this has existed prior to Common Core, but Common Core **sets into concrete** the fractured thinking and bad materialistic, progressive education of the past fifty years, producing an educational system that fails to develop discernment and wisdom.

Indoctrination by Omission

Much of the history of Western civilization's great inventors, writers, artists, statesmen and scientists steeped in the absolute truths of the Bible is missing, being replaced with modern moral relativists. American history favors Marxist Howard Zinn's heroes, not Paul Revere, John Adams, Ben Franklin, and Thomas Edison. The focus is on envy and class warfare. Even the innovation of hospitals and children's homes in the late nineteenth century by progressives such as the Roosevelt family does not receive their due. By ignoring certain things such as the rise of private Christian philanthropy, the student cannot include this as an option to solve a problem, since he knows nothing about it.

According to the Frankfurt School, their "political movement ... could only succeed when the individual believes that his or her actions are determined by not a personal destiny, but the destiny of the community in a world that has been abandoned by God."[2] Their success has resulted in *biblical illiteracy.* If there is no God, the government becomes god, changing the rules as it goes along. Arbitrary authority, and ultimately anarchy, will prevail. If the government does not follow the law, why should the citizens? Since the biblical God has been expunged from the discussion, citizens do not have to be accountable to a supreme being.

Biblical Knowledge

In identifying the important areas of study, Common Core never seriously suggests the Bible. Thus, when the Bible is no longer examined as the standard for truth, **man** becomes the measure of all things, and the most powerful of men are the ultimate measure. Early American history is replete with the understandings that without God and the Bible, there is no fixed point of truth from which to judge and order society. Wisdom is only achieved by integrating the education of the mind with absolutes and a knowledge base and merging it with the transcendent values of the heart and soul starting with biblical truth.

JANE ROBBINS POINTS OUT in *Common Core Hurts Education, Biblical Knowledge,* that David Coleman, the author of Common Core English Language Arts Standards,

> "advocates 'close reading' of a text, unencumbered by anything that might help the reader actually understand the text. For example,

he has trained English teachers to present the Gettysburg Address 'cold' with no instruction about the historical situation, the purpose of the address, or the scriptural allusions, and no dramatic reading of the speech. Students are to consider it as merely a collection of sentences that fell from the sky and arranged themselves on a page. [This minimalizes the questions of the soul, of good and evil and of purpose.] Apply that technique to Bible study. Christians should read the Scripture closely, of course, but in isolation from the breadth of biblical truth? How are we to truly understand Jesus' teachings without reference to the Mosaic Law that came before [Jesus]? ..."[3]

ENGLISH LANGUAGE STANDARDS in the Common Core Standards includes this exercise: "Interpret figures of speech (e.g., literary, biblical, and mythological allusions) in context."[4] However, most schools are preventing students from reading and studying the Bible, therefore how can they *interpret* a biblical figure of speech? How can they identify the numerous scriptural passages from the King James Bible in the writings of Shakespeare, George Washington, Samuel Coleridge, and others if they are not familiar with the Bible?

Another section of the standards instructs the student to "Analyze how an author draws on and transforms source material in a specific work (e.g., how Shakespeare treats a theme or topic from Ovid or the Bible or how a later author draws on a play by Shakespeare.)"[5] The allusion behind "the handwriting is on the wall" has little meaning to students who do not know the biblical story of Daniel and Belshazzar in the fifth chapter of Daniel.

How can they understand that the Declaration of Independence proclaims our rights come from a Creator who is the source of life, liberty and the pursuit of happiness when they do not know anything about the Creator of the Bible? Although pornographic literature is not banned in the classroom, the Bible is hard to find with most teachers believing it is off limits.

> The allusion behind "the handwriting is on the wall" has little meaning to students who do not know the biblical story of Daniel and Belshazzar.

Erwin W. Lutzer quotes Holocaust survivor, Viktor Frankl, in his book, "When A Nation Forgets

God: 7 Lessons We Must Learn from Nazi Germany":

> "The gas chambers of Auschwitz were the ultimate consequence of the theory that man is nothing but the product of heredity and environment – or as the Nazis like to say, 'Of blood and Soil.' I'm absolutely convinced that the gas chambers of Auschwitz, Treblinka and Majdanek were ultimately prepared not in some ministry or other of Berlin, but *rather at the desks and in the lecture halls of nihilistic scientists and philosophers.*[6] (Emphasis added.)

> **A nation that does not know where it came from, will never know where it is going.**

ANTI-AMERICAN HISTORY/SOCIAL STUDIES

By simply not mentioning certain subjects ... totalitarian propagandists have influenced opinion much more effectively than they could have done by the most ... compelling of logical rebuttals.[7] Aldous Huxley

A nation that does not know where it came from will never know where it is going. Today, our nation does not realize how close we are to Adolph Huxley's *Brave New World* where man is reduced to a robot, existing only for the use of a self-appointed cadre of progressive utopians and where each child has already been identified through massive data sorting and selection to meet the *greater good*. While American policy in education has historically focused on reading, writing and arithmetic, progressive/materialistic revisionists have claimed the high ground in historic re-interpretation, especially of American history and have been removing the underpinnings of what makes America free. The founders of the Frankfurt School would be delighted.

The face of Common Core can most vividly be seen in the College Board's release of the 98-page outline of the Advanced Placement curriculum for its AP U.S. History. Common Core lead writer, David Coleman, now heads the College Board.

Larry Krieger, author of leading U.S. History, World History and AP prep books, is critical of the College Board Framework and tests:

> "If history had a milk carton, Benjamin Franklin and Martin Luther King Jr.'s faces would both be listed as missing persons in this latest attempt to rewrite the past. And those two leaders aren't the only things absent from the Board's [College Board's SATs]

outline. 'There is no mention of Hitler, the Holocaust, D-Day, or other historic battles,' complains Christy Armbruster. "And you're not going to find Thomas Jefferson and the House of Burgesses and the cradle of democracy either,' chimed in test expert Larry Krieger.

" 'What you're going to find is our nation's founders portrayed as bigots who developed a belief in white superiority that was, in turn, derived from a strong belief in British racial and cultural superiority,' he explained. The proud tradition of religious liberty – the very thing that drove the Pilgrims to the new world – vanished from the text like the lost colony of Roanoke."[8]

"If the Framework virtually ignores the most important men and documents of American history, what does it find worthy of attention? **The answer is, pretty much anything that casts a negative light on our country.**"[9]

"As I read through the document, I saw a consistently negative view of American history that highlights oppressors and exploiters," Krieger said.[10]

"[T]he College Board Framework states that its goal is to train a new generation of students to become what it calls 'apprentice historians.' These 10th and 11th grade apprentice historians will read, interpret and argue about informational texts. The 98-page College Board document does not recommend a single work of literature. In addition, the just released College Board Sample Exam does not contain a single reference to a work of literature.

They have been taught to hate America.

"The content of the College Board document inculcates a consistently negative and superficial view of the American experience. For example, the College Board's anonymous authors dispatch World War II with the following two sentences: 'The mass mobilization of American society to supply troops for the war effort and a workforce on the home front ended the Great Depression and provided opportunities for women and minorities to improve their socioeconomic positions. Wartime experiences, such as the internment of Japanese Americans, challenges to civil liberties, debates over race and segregation, and the decision to drop the atomic bomb, raised questions about American values'."[11]

Already stories are flooding the Internet of students being told to " 'revise' the 'outdated' Bill of Rights by deleting and replacing two amendments, using the 'War on Terror' and the Patriot Act as a guide."[12] "Even more egregious is a Common Core workbook used by seventh-graders at Grant Middle School in Springfield, Illinois, which presents the Second Amendment to the United States Constitution as guaranteeing the right to bear **only arms that are registered**."[13]

The Messy Question

If several generations of students are indoctrinated with the anti-American worldview of Howard Zinn, what is to stop some of these citizens from traveling to the Middle East and taking up arms against America, especially since they have been taught to hate America?

According to Jihad Watch, "a college educated American citizen with a knack for computers is believed to be one of the men running the brutally effective ISIS social media operation, which is helping to attract hundreds of fighters from across the world – including the U.S., Britain, and Canada. Ahmad Abousamra, 32, was born in France and raised in the upscale Boston suburb of Stoughton. His father is a prominent endocrinologist at Massachusetts General Hospital. He attended the exclusive Xaverian Brothers Catholic High School and made the Dean's List at Northeastern University."[14]

Why would any person blessed with the freedoms in America become its enemy? What is being taught to our children in the classrooms is of grave importance and must bear closer inspection.

Because America is faced with a threat that has never before been imagined, giving students an understanding of their history of liberty that is based on eternal principles becomes important. When the culture and schools have stripped out the questions of an individual's purpose of the soul through years of promoting evolution, claiming man is nothing more than just sophisticated slime, individuals have become vulnerable to a sweeping ideology that purports to answer many of life's questions. All of us want a reason to be here, a purpose in life.

In our fast-moving, moral-relativistic world that proclaims there are no absolutes and there is no truth, the soul still searches for meaning and often wants "a cause."

These questions of the soul have been sabotaged by omission and untruths, especially the differences between America's founding Judeo-Christianity worldview and its chief antagonists: Islam, communism, socialism, and moral relativism.

Quite simply, textbooks and computers portray Islam as a religion of peace and leave out much of the fourteen hundred years of aggression. "On May 16 and 17 of 2012, *Channel One Network* (a national distributor of educational videos and newscasts viewed daily by over 8,000 middle and high schools) aired a two-part video series, titled 'Young and Muslim in America' and 'Islam in America'."[15] *American Thinker* author Larissa Scott complained, "Presenting an idealized, whitewashed image of Islam and its followers and showing how converting to Islam helps those who are lost and confused, this programming is nothing short of a disguised recruitment video pushing a religion in a public school setting."[16]

> We are endowed *by our Creator* with the blessings of life, liberty and the pursuit of happiness.

LIFE IS BOTH VALUABLE and sacred. Western Civilization's Judeo-Christian worldview of man in relation to truth, beauty, and goodness is a result of thousands of years of studying the humanities and philosophy that are based on absolutes, not moral relativism. The Bible teaches that God, who lovingly created man in His own image and gave him purpose, redeemed man's sinful nature. The first American schools were founded to teach children to read the Bible, and because this *was* American education from 1600 to the 1930s, discussions of personal identity and purpose thrived. In choosing the Judeo-Christian worldview and basing all education on biblical literacy, American children understood that they were created by God as our Declaration of Independence proclaims, "endowed by our Creator." They also understood the blessings of liberty, the pursuit of happiness, and that human life was sacred. That has changed today. The toxicity of a worldview devoid of a loving God has permeated the United States. There is little respect for life. Along with the loss of absolutes, we see an upsurge in bullying and cruelty among children. More importantly, man's quest to find purpose has been twisted. With this degradation of the human being and the cheapening of life comes the horrendous possibility of Americans succumbing to anti-life, hate teaching, murderous Islamists whose goal is worldwide domination, or other "isms" just as deadly. With the lack of facts about America's goodness, young unemployed men and women looking to find meaning in life are especially susceptible to the lure of Islamic propaganda.

Christianity and Islam – Life and Death

Few see the dividing line between living in a modern, 21st century, free America or reverting to the harsh, primitive subsistence of the seventh century Islamic past. Today's students do not understand that Christianity's sacredness of life is seriously being threatened by Islam's culture of death or even why it is important to understand the differences. It then becomes easy for them to succumb to the lure of power, and for some, a calling and a purpose for their lives. Beheadings, crucifixions, amputations, stonings, and mass slaughter of children, women, and Christian church congregations become purposeful and exciting, not wrong. Even seeing the seven year-old son of Sydney Jihadist Khaled Sharrout holding the severed head of a slain Syrian soldier while "wearing a pair of checked pants and a blue shirt with the insignia Polo Gold Kids"[17] does not receive condemnation.

> **If a foreign power had done to our educational system what has happened in the last generation, we would consider it an act of war.**

Clarion Project reports recently that Islamic State's Abdullah the Belgian appeared in a video on teaching children to kill. " 'For us, we believe that this generation of children is the generation of the caliphate. This generation will fight the infidels and apostates, the Americans and their allies, god willing. The right doctrine has been implanted in these children,' says an Islamic State member who is running a training camp for children. 'All of them love to fight for the building of the Islamic State and for the sake of god,' he says."[18]

If Americans no longer see the individual human being as created in the image of a loving, compassionate and forgiving God, sacred and holy, then what is to stop all hate and killing? Indeed, this becomes the *messy* question when we bow to political correctness and tolerance, fail to discuss the facts, and ignore the questions of the soul, of the eternal.

Little did America realize that by incorporating the goals of the Frankfurt School in the 1930s: "creation of racism offenses ... teaching of sex and homosexuality to children ... huge immigration to destroy identity ...

encouraging the breakdown of the family"[19] that we were being set up to embrace Shariah/Islamic/Jihadists.

When the 1984 report, *A Nation At Risk,* was released by the U.S. Department of Education, it stated, "If a foreign power had done to our educational system what has happened in the last generation, we would consider it an act of war." This was *before* Outcome Based Education and its stepchild Common Core had even been discovered by American parents and teachers and long before the textbooks whitewashed the Islamist march to rule to world. Common Core is disarming all citizens of the weapons of freedom.

Yet, it is no less an act of war today to let the federal government and its elites force Common Core onto the American people.

CHAPTER 4

THE SCIENCE STANDARDS

EDUCATING FOR AN AUTHENTIC WORLD OR FOR A WHIMSICAL ONE

*What happens to a nation that fails
to educate its next generation with
the facts that will enable them
to survive and prosper?*

4
THE SCIENCE STANDARDS

EDUCATING FOR AN AUTHENTIC WORLD OR FOR A WHIMSICAL ONE

IT IS CRITICAL that science education tell the truth; that science is not a consensus of opinions, but one of verification and replication of the facts, e.g., *the scientific method*. Dr. Michael Coffman[1], a noted forestry expert, respected scientist, and ecologist, delved into **Common Core's Next Generation Science Standards** (NGSS). This chapter is primarily his analysis of the overall thrust of their content.

Common Core's Next Generation Science Standards

Following on the heels of Goals 2000 and No Child Left Behind, Common Core intensifies the effort in American education to globalize education and promote the UN's *Agenda 21* with the Next Generation Science Standards.

Creating the Perfect Compliant Citizen

Over the past forty-plus years, the education cartel in the United States has given us Mastery Learning, Outcome-Based Education, Goals 2000, Careers Act, No Child Left Behind, and now Common Core. Each was designed to dazzle the uninformed with brilliant schemes to educate our children.

Concurrently, observers noted that these plans seemed to parallel the United Nations World Core Curriculum and Global 2000. Global 2000 was to prepare for the year 2000 by instituting a "worldwide collaborative process of unparalleled thinking, education and planning for a just and sustainable human world order."[2] The purpose of the World Core Curriculum is to, "Assist the child in becoming an integrated individual who can deal with personal dual who can deal with personal

education *for* sustainability

an agenda for action

education for sustainability contained numerous classroom suggestions and was part of the Sustainable America comprehensive program designed to move America into looking at everything through the lens of sustainability.

experience while seeing himself as part of 'the greater whole'." In other words, promote collectivism, so that the good of the group will "replace all limited, self-centered objectives, leading to group consciousness."

Agenda 21/Sustainable America

Agenda 21 was introduced to the world at the United Nations Conference on Environment and Development in Rio de Janeiro in 1992, and was signed by President George H. W. Bush. It had no legal teeth, so it was claimed that it would be harmless. **It is not.** It is a 40-chapter document that quite literally covers all human/environment and human/human interactions. If ever fully implemented, it is not a stretch to say it would allow a central government to control *every* activity of every *human being* on planet earth. Chapter 36 is **devoted to education, public awareness and training.** Outlined in this chapter is one of the purposes of *Agenda 21,* which is to "reorient education towards sustainable development." The goal continues: "Education [is] critical for achieving environmental and ethical awareness, values and attitudes, skills and behaviour consistent with sustainable development and for effective public participation in decision-making."[3]

Once President Clinton took office in 1993, he created the President's Council on Sustainable Development (PCSD) to implement *Agenda 21* in America. Under the authority of Clinton in 1996, the Council wrote the United State's version of *Agenda 21* called *Sustainable America.*

Sustainable America was broken into seven sub-documents in 1997, one of which was Public Linkage, Dialogue, and Education. Chapter 3 is dedicated to "Restructuring Formal Education" by integrating "environmental quality, economic prosperity, and social equity" into the standards for each discipline. Chapter 3 goes on to say: "Principles of sustainability can be used as a catalyst for innovation and **restructuring of educational institutions, curricula, and teacher training efforts**." (Emphasis added.)

Since 1996, billions of dollars have been spent by federal agencies to integrate *Sustainable America* (and by default *Agenda 21*) into every federal program using federal grants, including education. **That includes Common Core and Next Generation Science Standards (NGSS).**

Next Generation Science Standards

NGSS was developed by the National Research Council (the staff arm of the National Academy of Sciences) and the American Association for Advancement in Science. The NGSS web page states: "Quality science education is based on standards that are rich in content and practice, with aligned curricula, pedagogy, assessment, and teacher preparation and development." Like all progressive dogma, page after page of these empty platitudes allegedly justify the new science standards.

The NGSS were developed and follow the same template as Common Core. So much so they can eventually be merged seamlessly. *That is not coincidental.* An analysis of NGSS's treatment of climate change and sustainability clearly shows the fingerprints of *Agenda 21* and *Sustainable America.*

Modeling

The overriding feature of both subject areas (in fact, all subjects within NGSS) is the extraordinary dependence on *modeling* as standards [versus actual facts]. The extreme use of modeling almost guarantees a dumbed-down student [and reflects the political agenda behind it].

The new standards depend heavily, *in some cases almost exclusively,* on models at every grade level including kindergarten. The students not only use models developed or provided by the author of the textbook, but they are also required to create their own models. In the early grade levels, these are mostly pictorial, but increase in complexity through middle school. By high school the standards call for the use of an avalanche of math using complex models that would be beyond the cognitive ability of most high school students.

[Thomas Sowell notes, "The ultimate test of any theoretical model is not how loudly it is proclaimed but how well it fits the facts. ... (models do not show) other factors which go into temperatures on earth. It is not only the heat of the sunlight, but its duration, that determines how much heat builds up ... putting clouds into climate models is not simple, because the more the temperature rises, the more water evaporates, creating more clouds that reflect more sunlight back out into space. Such facts are well known, but reducing them to a specific and reliable formula that will predict global temperatures is something else. ..."[4]]

> **EXHIBIT A**
> **Human Sustainability Section**
> **High School Standards**
>
> K-8 experiences and progresses to using algebraic thinking and analysis, a range of linear and nonlinear functions including trigonometric functions, exponentials and logarithms, and computational tools for statistical analysis to analyze, represent, and model data. Simple computational simulations are created and used based on mathematical models of basic assumptions.
>
> § Create a computational model or simulation of a phenomenon, designed device, process, or system.
> § Use a computational representation of phenomena or design solutions to describe and/or support claims and/or explanations.

No one denies that models can help everyone understand complex relationships. Pictorial or simplified models are very important in lower grade levels where cognitive skills have not yet developed. However, when those models become complex mathematical constructs as is required at the NGSS high school level, the students will be so involved with the math and model intricacies that they will not, indeed cannot, see larger relationships. It is the old adage of not being able to see the forest for the trees. See Exhibit A.

Very few high school students will have the cogitative ability to understand, let alone do what this standard requires. What is extremely concerning about this standard is that most students will simply regurgitate on exams what the instructor tells them without understanding any of the principles underlying complex equations and models. In their haste to get the math right, they will certainly not understand it sufficiently to see any errors in overall logic to challenge the errors.

If the teacher has been indoctrinated into green theology, socialism (called progressivism in the U.S.), or politically-biased pseudoscience, which is increasingly the case, the instruction will be largely biased. That bias is what the student remembers. After all, the student reasons, it is supported by this complex mathematical construct or model they can't possibly understand, so it must be true. With enough reinforcement, by the time the student graduates from high school, this socialist and green bias becomes their worldview; the matrix of a person's most deeply held beliefs in what is real and not real. Once formed, it is almost impossible to change a person's worldview, even with overwhelming facts that show the worldview to be wrong.

A Worldview Based on Climate Models

A biased worldview is perfectly illustrated in President Obama's 2014 State of the Union Address when he proclaimed: "… the debate is settled. Climate change is a fact." ["Settled science" is self-contradicting.] Also astonishing is Secretary of State Kerry's statement to Indonesian students, civic leaders, and government officials: "We should not allow a tiny minority of shoddy scientists, and science and extreme ideologues, to compete with scientific facts … In a sense, climate change can now be considered the world's largest weapon of mass destruction, perhaps even, the world's most *fearsome weapon of mass destruction*."[5] (Italics added)

Global warming is the world's most fearsome weapon of mass destruction? Are global warming skeptics shoddy scientists and ideologues outside of scientific facts? [Many scientists] point out there is absolutely **no** empirical scientific evidence that man is causing global warming; many leading scientists are abandoning the "man-caused theory" and becoming skeptics.

Global Warming

Within the Weather and Climate section of High School Standards, students are supposed to be able to:

Analyze geoscience data and the results from global climate models to make an evidence-based forecast of the current rate of global or regional climate change and associated future impacts to Earth systems.

No empirical scientific evidence that man is causing global warming as the standards themselves insist has surfaced.

In other words, it is assumed the climate models accurately depict what is happening in the real world. **They do not**. The Standards then state that the student is supposed to construct models that:

build on K–8 experiences and progresses to using, synthesizing, and developing models to *predict and show relationships among variables between systems and their components* in the natural and designed world(s). (Italics added)

§ "Use a model to provide mechanistic accounts of phenomena."

The student is also required to analyze data:

and progress to introducing more detailed statistical analysis, the comparison of data sets for consistency, and the use of models to generate and analyze data.

§ Analyze data using computational models in order to make valid and reliable scientific claims.

Just how students are supposed to meet these science standards when the models they are using have failed miserably, even catastrophically, to predict future temperatures? This failure is precisely why models should be used sparingly and *never* as a final proof, as they are being used to prove man-caused global warming. Simply put, garbage-in garbage-out, no matter how sincere the modelers.

Empirical Based Science

There are numerous *correct* science standards in the NGSS. One of them is the standard listed for every grade level that science is based on empirical evidence. *Empirical evidence is real, observable relationships and data.* **Models are not empirical evidence.** Although empirical data is usually used in developing these models, they are in reality mathematical constructs existing in their own world, divorced from the real world. They are merely supposed to predict the real world. ***Yet, they are the only evidence of man-caused global warming.*** Again, this is a classic reason why models should not be used as the primary teaching standard of anything at any grade level. It is entirely a political theory based on non-scientific models that could cost the United States economy trillions of dollars.

This conflict between the use of models and the standard that science is based in empirical evidence establishes a schizophrenic dichotomy between standards. It is perhaps the fatal flaw in the NGSS and clearly exposes the link back to *Agenda 21* and *Sustainable America*. This simply cannot be an oversight on the part of writers of the NGSS.

This schizophrenic dichotomy can do nothing but cause frustration and confusion for the students, leaving them feeling stupid. By constantly reinforcing potential errors as truth, thereby creating confusion at every grade level, the student's worldview is being formed using totally incorrect conclusions. These conclusions will then be almost impossible to overcome when they are adults. They do serve, however, as a perfect tool for indoctrination and dumbing down. If there were any doubt that NGSS is deliberately indoctrinating students on global warming, the Disciplinary Core Ideas of the Human Sustainability section proves it:

Weather and Climate

§ Current models predict that, although future regional climate changes will be complex and varied, *average global temperatures will continue to rise. The outcomes predicted by global climate models strongly depend on the amounts of human-generated greenhouse gases added to the atmosphere each year and by the ways in which these gases are absorbed by the ocean and biosphere.* (Italics added.)

In actuality, the real-world temperature data shows just the ***opposite*** of this Disciplinary Core Idea. There has been ***no*** statistical warming since 1997, eighteen years ago. In addition, a graph of 90 Climate Models shows that the actual surface temperature has gone ***down*** slightly. This is the same data the United Nations' Intergovernmental Panel on Climate Change (IPCC) uses.

Alarmists claim that seventeen years (1997-2014) is not long enough to provide a valid trend. They never admit the warming period from 1977 to 1997 was only twenty years. Yet, they claim that those twenty years is irrefutable evidence the world is about to melt. It was certainly enough to spend hundreds of billions of dollars and a huge attempt to pass Cap and Trade or carbon tax legislation that would have seriously harmed the United States economy had the legislation passed. Yet, real science is strongly suggesting that we are going into decades of global cooling— perhaps severe global cooling.

Common Core Science Standards do not reflect man's superior position in the plant and animal kingdom.

[Common Core promotes fears of catastrophic global warming based solely on computer climate models, but fails to note that the models are invalidated by the fact that actual temperature observations show only a small fraction of the warming they simulate and no warming for the last eighteen-plus years. This demonstrates that CO_2's warming effect is much less than the models assume and leaves no rational basis for the fears or for any policy based on them.[6]]

Sustainability

The science standards of every grade level require some level of exposure to the need to live sustainably. Fifteen-plus years ago, no one had ever heard of the word sustainability, at least not as it is used in the science standards. The fact that sustainability is a standard of every grade level is a good indication of how thoroughly *Sustainable America* has penetrated NGSS. Like models, sustainability is not a science and should never be included in NGSS. At best, it is a social construct in which various science applications can be, but not necessarily, made. Even in kindergarten, students are taught to "communicate solutions that will reduce the impact of humans on the land, water, air, and/ or other living things in the local environment."

The lesson learned by the students: **Humans cause environmental destruction, and we must learn to sacrifice our conveniences to protect the environment.**

The Next Generation Science Standards focus on reducing the impact of humans on the land, water, air, etc., and do not include any standard that reflects man's superior position in the plant and animal kingdom. This opens the door to the pantheistic belief that man is no better than plants or animals, or worse, plants and animals are equal or even superior to man. This has and is leading to the nihilistic belief that man is the problem and the only solution is to get rid of man. The entire set of science standards leads to a sense of *doom* and *hopelessness* and suggests that only a radical change in our cultural behavior will provide any hope of salvation. **This is very intentional.**

Following are sections from the "Human Impacts" section of the standards. An instruction is given in the standards with a "Clarification Statement" written in red after it. By middle school, students should understand how to:

> **"Apply scientific principles to design a method for monitoring and minimizing a human impact on the environment.**
>
> **Clarification Statement:** Examples of the design process include examining human environmental impacts, assessing the kinds of solutions that are feasible, and designing and evaluating solutions that could reduce that impact. Examples of human impacts can include water usage (such as the withdrawal of water from streams and aquifers or the construction of dams and levees), land usage **(such as urban development, agriculture, or the removal of wetlands),** and pollution (such as of the air, water, or land)."

> **"Construct an argument supported by evidence for how increases in human population and per-capita consumption of natural resources impact Earth's systems.**
>
> **Clarification Statement:** Examples of evidence include grade-appropriate databases on human populations and the rates of consumption of food and natural resources (such as freshwater, mineral, and energy). Examples of impacts can include changes to the appearance, composition, and structure of Earth's systems as well as the rates at which they change. The consequences of increases in human populations and consumption of natural resources are described by science, **but science does not make the decisions for the actions society takes."**

By focusing exclusively on the **negative impacts of humans**, the standard becomes pure dogma. It is designed to pull the student into a "sustainable worldview" **in which human activity must be heavily regulated to stop the damage.** The standard is only part of the picture—a very negative part designed to subtly teach the student that humans are the problem and the enemy of every other living and non-living entity on earth. To the extent that humans must take care of the earth (called stewardship), these standards are partially correct. Even the Bible calls mankind to do that. But the Bible also tells mankind to subdue nature. One only needs to realize that nature constantly fights any change to understand why. Just try growing a productive garden without subduing the weeds. Subduing nature is exactly the opposite of what *Agenda 21/Sustainable America* and these standards call for.

Farmers, foresters, ranchers, and all people who must manage the environment for human benefits also know that **mankind can actually benefit nature. Altering forest and rangeland biodiversity to benefit mankind, for instance, can also benefit ecosystem health.** While old-growth forests have a place in a forested ecosystem, they are usually barren of biodiversity. When harvesting parts of old-growth forests, not only does man benefit from the lumber or veneer harvested, but also ecosystem health and vigor skyrockets as biodiversity greatly increases, because new habitat is created for many new species. Another benefit that is not mentioned is that intensive agriculture can grow more crops on fewer acres, releasing former agriculture land back to a natural condition. Nor does any standard mention the "green revolution" that occurred in the 1940s-1960s. Led by Norman Borlaug, it is credited with saving over a billion people from starvation worldwide.

Property Rights vs. Urban Planning

Because the standards *imply only negative impacts*, once again leaving the student with a sense of undefined nihilism, they convey that humans are always doing damage to the environment, and they must be stopped. To do this, **property rights must be severely restricted, if not eliminated**.

"Urban planning" is a key standard used in reducing human impact. What is not said is that urban planning is the primary means of controlling property rights to become "sustainable." It includes urban growth boundaries, high-density housing, smaller dwellings, smaller and fewer cars, more public transportation like very expensive light-rail, fewer electronic conveniences, and much more in order to reduce fossil fuel requirements. In effect, the **government** will control *all development and land use*.

This principle of urban planning was established by the UN in their Habitat I in 1979 and continues in *Agenda 21* and *Sustainable America*: "The provision of decent dwellings and healthy conditions for the people can only be achieved if land is used in the interests of society as a whole. Public control of land use is therefore indispensable ..." [*Sustainable America* was created specifically to help teachers teach *Agenda 21* in the classroom.] Although not specifically stated, the Next Generation Science Standards fit perfectly within this concept.

The attack on private property rights gets much, much worse if the concept of sustainability is ever realized. For instance, in High School-ESS3-2, the statement "developing best practices for agricultural soil use" is interpreted in the UN Convention on Biological Diversity (Chapter 15 of *Agenda 21*) as minimal impact to the environment.

> **The Standards convey that humans are always doing damage to the environment, and they must be stopped.**

Minimal agriculture would be found in what are called "Buffer Zones" that protect the core wilderness areas found in interconnecting corridors and reserves. [*Agenda 21* specified that] *the core wilderness areas and corridors would occupy* **40 to 50 percent** *of the United States and the buffer zones about* **30 to 40 percent**. *Intensive agriculture could only be practiced on the remaining* **20 to 30 percent** *of the land area, which would also include cities, towns and villages.*

This sounds insane, but the treaty came within an hour of being ratified in the U.S. Senate in 1994 when its outrageous, anti-human requirements were exposed by this author [Michael Coffman].[7]

The Importance of Private Property Rights

By emphasizing the need to protect the environment at any cost, property rights are stripped from citizens. Neither *Agenda 21* nor *Sustainable America* can be implemented without taking private property rights. It is criminal that property rights are not considered at all in the NGSS.

According to the Fraser Institute's *Economic Freedom of the World 2013 Annual Report*, the United States had the strongest legally protected private property in the world until the 1980s. The United States is now ranked 38th in the world.

At the same time, social and big government regulations (which are in fact, restrictions on property rights) also began to expand exponentially until we now have between 3,000 to 4,000 new federal regulations proposed *every month*. The Competitive Economic Institute has determined that these regulations now cost the United States $1.8 trillion annually. The United States dropped from second place in world ranking for the fewest burdensome regulations in 1980 (behind Hong Kong) to 18th place in 2011. Some regulations are necessary, but the majority attempt to achieve some social goal that is counterproductive.

Recap

There exists a one-to-one relationship of carbon dioxide emissions and the health of our economy. Next Generation Science Standards make carbon dioxide and urban planning two social centerpieces of its standards to ostensibly prevent global warming and the destruction of biodiversity. Both are social goals, not science. By focusing on social issues, the ***NGSS indoctrinate graduating seniors to believe that federal and state governments must have the right to control the economy and our daily lives, lest we all die.*** History shows that governments need little encouragement to increasingly take more and more liberties from the people until they control what they can and cannot do.

That process is already well under way in America. Government control of property rights, including the right to emit carbon, is exactly what *Agenda 21* and *Sustainable America* are designed to do. It is exactly why global warming and environmental planning are the centerpieces of the entire global political agenda, and why they won't let the issue die politically or in the Next Generation Science Standards.

By focusing on computer models, fallacious global warming and sustainability rather than facts and principles, the NGSS will continue the rapid deterioration of education.

~ ~ ~ ~ ~

Woven throughout the Science Standards is the idea the Marxist Frankfurt School promotes that man is only valuable if he serves the state. A steady dose of science teaching that man is a plague, not a blessing, has caused many students to feel hopeless as they lament over their *shared space* or *polluting footprint*. The recruiters for ISIS are targeting this hopelessness with increasing success.

CHAPTER 5

MIND/THOUGHT CONTROL

MEASURING AND TRACKING

Without economic security,
the love of servitude cannot possibly
come to existence.[1] Aldous Huxley

5
MIND/THOUGHT CONTROL

MEASURING AND TRACKING

IN ORDER FOR THE PROGRESSIVE ideology of the Science, History, English and Math Standards to become the thoughts of all students, a system of mind/thought control must be established.

The proposed measuring and the tracking of student emotions, using biometrics, such as retina scans, obtained while students take a test on a school computer, is in addition to the immense data collection already amassed by government entities such as Social Security, IRS tax records, local property deeds, health records, etc. In the private sector, businesses use *voice-profiling* devices that sort incoming phone calls, which then identify the caller based on their emotions, i.e., angry, frustrated, etc.

Jane Robbins of American Principles Project discovered that *The Gordon Report* "shares a philosophy with a recent report from the Office of Educational Technology at the U.S. Department of Education: 'Promoting Grit, Tenacity, and Perseverance – Critical Factors for Success in the 21st Century'."[2] One section of that report examines how to measure the intangibles that lead to academic success. It found that although currently impractical for the classroom, 'some of the most promising new directions are educational data mining and affective computing.' Educational data mining is defined as collecting and analyzing data concerning 'behavioral variables' such as 'time on task, help-seeking, revisiting a problem,' etc. **Here's the alarming issue**: Affective computing is defined as 'development of systems and devices that can recognize, interpret, process, and simulate aspects of human affect. Emotional or physiological variables can be used to enrich the understanding and usefulness of behavioral indicators. Discrete emotions particularly relevant to reactions to challenge – such as interest, frustration, anxiety, and boredom – may be measured through analysis of facial expressions, EEG brain wave patterns, skin conductance, heart rate variability, posture, and eye-tracking'."[3]

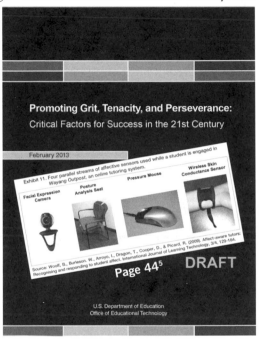

"Joy Pullmann of the Heartland Institute, discovered a report by the U.S. Department of Education revealing that Common Core's data mining includes 'using cameras to judge facial expressions, an electronic seat that judges posture, a pressure-sensitive computer mouse, and a biometric wrap on kids' wrists'."[4]

BATTLE FOR THE BRAIN

"Suppose that an authoritarian government decides to embark on a program of curricular reform, with the explicit goal of indoctrinating the nation's high school students."[6] Cass Sunstein

In *Open Brain, Insert Ideology*, Cass Sunstein notes, "New research, from Davide Cantoni of the University of Munich and several co-authors, shows that recent curricular reforms in China, explicitly designed to transform students' political views, have *mostly worked*. The findings offer remarkable evidence about the potential influence of the high school curriculum on what students end up thinking …"[7] Even though Sunstein concludes his observations with a warning, he notes, "In a democratic country with a flourishing civil society, a high degree of pluralism, and ample room for disagreement and dissent – like the U.S. – it may well be harder to use the curriculum to change the political views of young people. *But even in such societies, high schools probably have a significant ability to move students toward what they consider 'a correct worldview, a correct view on life, and a correct value system'.*"[8] (Emphasis added.)

Cass Sunstein, "the former administrator of the White House Office of Information and Regulatory Affairs [Obama Presidency], is the Robert Walmsley University professor at Harvard Law School and a *Bloomberg View* columnist. Sunstein is also the director of the law school's program on behavioral economics and public policy."[9]

Sunstein's comments immediately raise the question: *What is the purpose of education in a free society?* Is it to **indoctrinate** the student with a particular worldview **or** to **teach** and **mentor** each child so that he will become unique and independent, creative and innovative, wise and moral as he is schooled in the absolute truths and wisdom of the ages? This raises the secondary question of: *Who has the power to decide?*

A careful reading of the Sunstein article detects a respect for the Chinese system of successful indoctrination, with an implied concern that America's current progressive ideology might not prevail. Taken in context with Cass Sunstein's other writings, his worldview (an FDR progressive[10]) is being amply reflected in Common Core, the current title of federal takeover of education. What Sunstein does not explain is how the Chinese have succeeded in indoctrinating students. Nor does he discuss how far along American education is on this same path.

The study Sunstein references is called "Curriculum and Ideology." The author's summary states, "We study the casual effects of school curricula on students' stated beliefs and attitudes. We exploit a major textbook reform in China that was rolled out … with the explicit intention of shaping youths' *ideology* … study under the new curriculum is robustly associated with changed views on political participation … and a more skeptical view of free markets."[11] (Emphasis added.)

American Education looks to China

How has American education undertaken progressive ideological indoctrination versus developing independent thinkers? Following in China's footsteps, does it have the technology to enforce it? Perhaps one of the most telling statements was recently published in *The Wall Street Journal* article about a young Chinese mother who was trying to take her daughter and leave China. Among other reasons, she did not want her daughter to be educated in China because her daughter "... has a talent for music, art and storytelling that Ms. Sun fears China's *test-driven schools won't nurture.*"[12] (Emphasis added.) Why the reference to "test-driven schools"? It is the assessments and tests that are the enforcers of not only changed views on political ideology but the success of the curriculum. A well-functioning totalitarian system and its power depend upon controlling *what* information is available and *who* makes the decisions. If schools use assessments for thought-control, *slanting* the information while at the same time *omitting* critical areas, current and future generations will be both ignorant and misinformed of facts and understandings necessary for the survival of freedom, which will *make totalitarian control possible.* Bottom line, it will be a dictator's delight.

In Ms. Sun's case, she saw the curriculum as choking out the creativity in her daughter. In the Chinese system, all education is not only top-down and assessment-driven, but for years, dossiers have been maintained on every child at the national level and contain immense amounts of personal information assembled around school records, making it easier to mold the child to the authoritarian government's purposes.

As far back as 1992, the *New York Times* carried an article called "Personal File and Worker Yoked for Life," describing how "as part of [Communist] China's complex system of social control and surveillance, the authorities keep a dangan (or file) on virtually everyone except peasants." Each dangan starts with school records, grade transcripts and "performance evaluations." "A file is opened on each urban citizen when he or she enters elementary school, and it shadows the person throughout life, moving onto high school, college and employer. Particularly for officials, students, professors and Communist Party members, the dangan contains political evaluations that affect career prospects and permission to leave the country. ... The dangan affects promotions and job opportunities, and it is difficult to escape from because any prospective employer is supposed to examine an applicant's dangan before making a hiring decision. The dangan is part of a web of social controls that insure order in China."[13]

> **A well-functioning totalitarian system and its power depend upon controlling *what* information is available and *who* makes the decisions.**

The history of mankind is the story of the struggle over power and who makes the decisions. Today that threat is manifesting itself through technology, especially technology resting in the hands of government agents. The battle over Common Core will determine who wins the future.

Microchips/Biometrics

Consider these stories that illustrate what we're up against.

FOX NEWS: SEPTEMBER 12, 2012, SAN ANTONIO, TX: "A Texas school district's plan to track students with microchips implanted in mandatory IDs has at least one parent charging [that] it's an invasion of his daughter's privacy. Beginning in the middle of October [2012], roughly 4,300 students at John Jay High School and Anson Jones Middle School in San Antonio will be required to wear the ID cards that utilize radio frequency identification. The card … will transmit location information via microchip to electronic readers throughout the campuses …"[14] Alert parents temporarily stopped this program.

CREATORS SYNDICATE, MAY 30, 2014, COLUMNIST MICHELLE MALKIN: "… BMI [body mass indexes] report card promoters are pushing for far more radical data-mining intrusion. A little-noticed study published in the journal *Health Affairs* a few years ago on '**state surveillance of childhood obesity**' proposes getting around federal family privacy protections by declaring obesity a '**public health threat**' at every state level. This would allow agencies to invoke '**public health protection powers**' to allow unfettered sharing of student BMI data."[15] Already, notices are coming home telling some parents, "Because [y]our daughter's body-mass index is 'very low' [you] 'should make certain' that she 'is eating a healthy diet that includes the appropriate number of calories.'"[16]

FOX NEWS, JANUARY 31, 2014, WISCONSIN: A middle school in Marinette, Wisconsin, got a group of "fifth through eighth grade students to play the *game* called 'Cross the Line'. Parents say their children were asked personal questions like, do your parents drink and has anyone in your family been in jail? Students were also asked to step forward if they answered 'yes' to any of the questions." As part of the *game*, the students were asked questions like: Do you cut yourself? Have you ever wanted to commit suicide? Do you or your parents do drugs?[17]

LOCAL CBS, TAMPA FL, JUNE 3, 2013, POLK COUNTY, FL:

"Parents are in shock after finding out three schools in Florida had been using iris scanners to collect biometric data about their children, without their permission. ... Proponents of the program say the technology presents an easier way to keep tabs on students than the current system which requires them to wear ID badges while on campus."[18]

THE NEW AMERICAN, OCTOBER 2012, WASHINGTON, D.C.:

"The Department of Education released a brief entitled 'Enhancing, Teaching and Learning Through Educational Data Mining and Learning Analytics', in which the following was stated about data mining procedures, 'A student learning database (or other big data repository) stores time-stamped student input and behaviors captured as students work within the system. A predictive model combines demographic data (from an external student information system) and learning/behavior data from the student learning database to track a student's progress and make predictions about his or her future behaviors or performance, such as future course outcomes and dropouts'."[19]

For a much more detailed examination of the big data threat to Americans, see Pioneer Institute's, May 2014, White Paper #114, "Cogs in the Machine, Big Data, Common Core, and National Testing" by Emmett McGroarty, Joy Pullmann, and Jane Robbins.[20]

Although the words **assessments** and **tests** are often used interchangeably, it is important to realize that **assessments** measure behavioral changes moving from one point to another with a goal in mind, e.g., how much further was Johnny able to run in a minute from last year to this? **Tests** measure acquisition of knowledge with a right or wrong answer, e.g., what is the capital of the State of Kansas? Most activities called **testing** in schools are actually **assessments.** They do not determine how much or what someone **knows**. They measure how far Johnny has moved along a pre-determined set of behavioral outcomes.

Adaptive Learning Assessments

KNEWTON'S TECHNOLOGY: *Newsweek, July 7, 2013,* asked, "What if You Could Learn Everything?" The article asked the reader to, "Imagine every student has a tireless personal tutor, an artificially intelligent and inexhaustible companion that magically knows everything, knows the student, and helps her learn what she needs to know." *Newsweek* explains that a system does exist to do this and it is called *adaptive learning.* "Adaptive learning is an

> **Assessments measure behavioral changes moving from one point to another with a goal in mind. Tests measure acquisition of knowledge with a right or wrong answer.**

increasingly popular catchphrase denoting educational software that customizes its presentation of material from moment to moment based on the user's input. It's being hailed as a 'revolution' by both venture capitalists and big established education companies."[21]

The article is an in-depth look at Jose Ferreira, the founder of Knewton, an education technology startup company. To really understand why adaptive learning can be dangerous, here is more of the *Newsweek* article:

"Starting this fall, Knewton's technology will be available to the vast majority of the nation's colleges and universities and K-12 school districts through new partnerships with three major textbook publishers: Pearson, MacMillan, and Houghton Mifflin Harcourt. And Ferreira's done all this even though he says neither his investors nor his competition—to say nothing of the public or the press—really understand what Knewton can do.

"But here's the vision. Within five or 10 years, the paper textbook and mimeographed worksheet will be dead. Classroom exercises and homework—text, audio, video, and games—will have shifted entirely to the iPad or equivalent. And adaptive learning will help each user find the exact right piece of content needed, in the exact right format, at the exact right time, based on previous patterns of use."[22]

This next section has critical implications.

"When a textbook publisher like Pearson loads its curriculum into Knewton's platform, each piece of content—it could be a video, a test question, or a paragraph of text—is tagged with the appropriate concept or concepts.

"Let's say your school bought the Knewton-powered MyMathLab online system, using the specific curriculum based on, say, Lial's Basic College Mathematics 8e. When a student logs on to the system, she first takes a simple placement test or pretest from the book, which has been tagged with the relevant 'atomic concepts.' As a student reads the text or watches the video and answers the questions, Knewton's system is 'reading' the student as well—timing every second on task, tabulating every keystroke, and constructing a profile of learning style: hesitant or confident? Guessing blindly or taking her time? Based on the student's answers, and what she did before getting the answer, 'we can tell you to the percentile, for each concept: how fast they learned it, how well they know it, how long they'll retain it, and how likely they are to learn other similar concepts that well,' says Ferreira. 'I can tell you that to a degree that most people don't think is possible. It sounds like space talk.' By watching as a student interacts with it, the platform extrapolates, for example, 'If you learn concept No. 513 best in the morning between 8:20 and 9:35 with 80 percent text and 20 percent rich media and no more than 32 minutes at a time, well, then the odds are you're going to learn every one of 12 highly correlated concepts best that same way'.

"The platform forms a personalized study plan based on that information and decides what the student should work on next, feeding the student the appropriate new pieces of content and continuously checking the progress. [Emphasis added.] A dashboard shows the student how many 'mastery points' have been achieved and what to do next. Teachers, likewise, can see exactly which concepts the student is struggling with, and not only whether the homework problems have been done, but also how many times each problem was attempted, how many hints were needed, and whether the student looked at the page or opened up the video with the relevant explanation.

"The more people use the system, the better it gets; and the more you use it, the better it gets for you."[23]

More information on Ferreira's system can be found in a *YouTube* video, (https://www.youtube.com/watch?v=Lr7Z7ysDluQ) on which he "shares his vision for a future where every student receives a truly personalized curriculum best suited to his or her needs. Knewton collects millions of data points about student users in order to provide them with more effective timing and content to enhance learning."[24]

Adaptive assessments ramp up the discussion over *what is being taught and then assessed for* and most importantly, *who decides*. If those in charge of the assessments should decide to manipulate the assessment for political, religious, and philosophical worldviews, what is to stop them?

How would the parent or teacher know, because only the student moving through the sets of questions could document the direction of the assessment? There are no paper documents or test booklets. The computer-directed and controlled assessments are the perfect cover for raw power. Consequently, an examination of what is already in the pipeline of Common Core texts, homework assessments, and federal proclamations is a must.

As far back as 1993, Missouri's Outstanding Schools Act of 1993 specified that an outstate consortium develop and help implement assessment for Missouri. Missouri contracted with the New Standards Project (Co-chair Marc Tucker[25]) and by summer of 1995 had already piloted assessments and trained a number of lead teachers. It is instructive to examine some of the pilot assessments used:

TRASH TROUBLES is the title of one of the language arts assessments for fourth graders. The assessment involves teaching activities for three to four days, and then the written assessment on the fifth day. The children are subjected to videos, poems, and stories about the problems of trash in the United States. They are to write down their reactions as they go along and use these notes for their *test*.

The test consists of writing a letter to a "person or group in your community telling them about the community's trash problems and what you think should be done about them." The *pilot* for the teachers then includes a number of written responses from the 9-year olds as well as their notes.

> The *best* answers always directed the solution to a government agency, a subtle way to reinforce the idea that government solves all problems.

A politically correct answer is the goal. The top score of four is given to the students that show by their answer that they will be good "change agents" for society.

It is appalling how fearful some of the children were after three to four days of exposure to "Trash Troubles." Some children in pilot test studies near the Rio Grande River in Texas noted, "More babies are going to be born without a brain and more people are going to be blind." Another child said, "When the women have ther (sic) babies, the babies don't have brains." This student had obviously been told that the mothers drank the water of the Rio Grande that was polluted. Other children were troubled that they would be buried by trash by the time they grew up and worried about the dismal future.

Nowhere in any of the scoring rubrics or instructions to the teachers, much less to the students, is there a glimpse of a private sector or free enterprise solution. The best answers always directed the solution to a government agency, a subtle way to reinforce the idea that government solves all problems.

Back to Building the Data

With the 2009 Federal Stimulus package came federal enforcement of uniform state student data. Forbidden for years to build an educational national database, the federal government circumvented it with the requirement that each state match its data to all the other states if they wanted to receive any of the millions of stimulus money given through the U.S. Department of Education. Known as the *Statewide Longitudinal Data Systems* its goal was to "… provide grants to states to design, develop, and implement statewide P-20 longitudinal data systems to capture, analyze, and use student data from preschool to high school, college, and the workforce. … To receive State Fiscal Stabilization Funds, a state must provide an assurance that it will establish a longitudinal data system that includes the 12 elements described in the America COMPETES Act, and any data system developed with Statewide longitudinal data system funds must include at least these 12 elements."[26]

When the federal rules about privacy on student information were changed, it allowed just about anyone access. Dr. Paul Kengor, executive director of The Center for Vision and Values, posits, "We're facing, in essence, unchecked data collection as part of a significant and sweeping federal educational mandate."[27] As part of the building of the data, any child taking the ACT is required to fill in an extensive questionnaire (even before opening the test) that includes identifying the student's participation in:

- "ethnic organizations,
- political organizations,
- religious organizations,
- hours a week … worked for pay, and
- religious affiliations"

(Forty religious choices are listed, among them Muslim, Baha'i, Buddhist, Baptist, Hindu, and Reformed Church in America.)

In the "Interest Inventory," the student is asked if he dislikes, is indifferent to or likes 72 different areas such as "#10. Campaign for a political office; #49. Read about the origin of the earth, sun, and stars; #64. Explain legal rights to people."[28] ACT's "Interest Inventory" builds the database, based on

> **Education becomes a narrowing thought-control system rather than an avenue of building a base of knowledge that continues to radiate outward.**

workforce development and career development goals. The student is treated as a *human resource*, not a unique individual with his own ideas of what he wants to do or be.

inBloom, a cloud data system, was working to take myriad points of data on an individual and tailor it to not only predict future behavior, but to have a say-so in that future behavior. Bill Gates poured millions into this data collection in furtherance of his huge investment in seeing Common Core succeed. *inBloom* failed due to parental outcry over unsecure student data; yet other cloud systems are taking its place. At first glance, those dealing with a wayward child would agree that behavioral change is needed; yet where is the line drawn? Should mom, dad, teacher, and the counselor assess the situation and suggest changes? **Or** should Big Brother make the decisions based on data mining and retain the power of college and job access for that student? Who is being paid by powerful interests to provide workers for a particular project/industry? What if Big Brother, an anonymous busy body, decides that this particular student's worldview is a threat to the prevailing power elite and that the student should not be allowed to become a leader, but be relegated to the drone worker force? **When data becomes the major determining point of advancing through life, those that control the data rule supreme.**

By defining every tidbit of perceived beliefs into a separate outcome as Jose Ferreira, CEO of Knewton, describes and then using a computer to reinforce the acceptance of this or to change the beliefs, education becomes a narrowing thought-control system rather than an avenue of building a base of knowledge that continues to radiate outward.

The goal of a thought-control education system is not to produce independent, creative innovative thinkers, but to turn out complacent, obedient wards of the state that will be funneled into jobs without protest.

CHAPTER 6

SETTING THE STAGE FOR COMMON CORE

THREE PIECES OF LEGISLATION

*How did we get to this point
of government control over individual
students, and in particular,
their careers and jobs?*

6
SETTING THE STAGE FOR COMMON CORE

THREE PIECES OF LEGISLATION

THE AGENDA OF THE MARXISTS of the Frankfurt School and Antonio Gramsci was moved forward with federal legislation. 1994 brought about three primary pieces of federal educational legislation and set up the mechanism of power necessary to enforce a set of federally-determined attitudes, beliefs and behaviors for all Americans, starting with the children and ending with the worker when he leaves the workforce at retirement. While Americans were thinking academic education based on facts, what they were getting was indoctrination based on opinions.

The three primary vehicles for the "revolution of mind and body" were as follows:

- **SCHOOL-TO-WORK (STWO)** became law on May 4, 1994, as Public Law 103-239

- **GOALS 2000** signed into law March 31, 1994, by President Clinton as Public Law 103-227

- **IMPROVING AMERICA'S SCHOOLS ACT** of 1994 (**IASA**) became law on October 20, 1994, as Public Law 103-382

These three pieces of legislation are interwoven and dependent, and when combined, they broaden the reach of each other. The "voluntary" goals of GOALS 2000 remained voluntary until IASA was passed. By tying the money to acceptable standards, IASA, in effect, ruled out any opting-out by local schools. Since 90% of the nation's schools receive some kind of federal aid for *at-risk* students (which is what IASA funds), cutting off the money would create major problems for local schools.

Furthermore, these three bills represented a major push toward a federal classroom. This may sound well and good until one looks at the mandates that came with these pieces of legislation.

Common Core brings about the federalized classroom, which de-emphasizes basic skills. As stated in the opening pages of the 1994 IASA bill, "[B]asic skills" that "empha[size] repetitive drill and practice"[1] are "disproven theory."[2] Learning sounds and symbols such as those used when teaching phonetic-based reading, mastering multiplication tables by rote in mathematics, and memorizing facts in history (such as when the Civil War occurred) is considered obsolete by IASA. If memorizing facts such as these are obsolete, what do they call *Standards*? In its final version, IASA dropped the specific language above due to a great outcry from the citizens, but alludes to it with the language, "Use of low-level tests [memorization of multiplication tables, etc.] that are not aligned with schools' curricula fails to provide adequate information about what children know and can do and encourages curricula and instruction that focus on the low level skills [phonics, math tables, history dates, and places] measured by such tests."[3]

A careful reading of both GOALS 2000 and IASA uncovers the "politically correct" set of attitudes, values and behaviors necessary to create a servitude class of people. These go under the cover of "Standards/goals/expectations/objectives/frameworks." Simply stated, goals are broader than standards. Frameworks, expectations and objectives are more specific than goals and standards.

SCHOOL TO WORK/WORKFORCE DEVELOPMENT

The love of servitude cannot be established except as a result of a deep, personal revolution in human minds and bodies. To bring about that revolution we require ... [A] fully developed science of human differences, **enabling government managers to assign any given individual** to his or her proper place in the social and economic hierarchy.[4] Aldous Huxley (Emphasis added.)

In 1932, Aldous Huxley penned the classic, *Brave New World*. Ask anyone if it is a classic and they will answer yes; ask them if they have read it, and they will probably answer no. Yet, this book says much about what is happening today. *Brave New World* describes man's creation of an utopian society where there is no strife, hunger, or unknowns, and it explains the factors necessary to get there and make it work. Revised after World War II, Huxley wrote in the Foreward to the 1946 edition,

> *A really efficient totalitarian state would be one in which the all-powerful executive of political bosses and their army of managers control a population of slaves who do not have to be coerced, because they love their servitude.* **To make them love it is the task assigned,** *in present-day totalitarian states, to ministries of propaganda [i.e., movies, television, etc.] newspaper editors and* **schoolteachers.**[5] (Emphasis added.)

Huxley continues, "A love of servitude cannot be established except as the result of a deep, personal **revolution in human minds and bodies.**"[6] (Emphasis added.)

Brave New World is the story of a civilization where that revolution of human minds and bodies has occurred. It describes a future that many believed was partially fulfilled by Hitler's fascist/socialist Third Reich. Many of *Brave New World's* ideas were put into motion during the Third Reich, so Huxley rewrote his introduction attempting to distinguish between good totalitarian governments and bad. He said, "The people who govern the *Brave New World* may not be sane (in what may be called the absolute sense of the word); but they are not madmen, and their aim is not anarchy but social stability. It is *in order to achieve stability* that they carry out, by scientific means, the ultimate, personal, really revolutionary revolution."[7] (Emphasis added.) Americans would do well to read it carefully today for its relevance, particularly with what is happening in the classroom. As Abraham Lincoln is reputed to have said:

> **What is happening in today's classroom is the politics of the next generation.**

If Lincoln is correct, that the teachings in today's classroom produce the future culture, then we **must** take time to find out what those teachings are and how they are being imprinted on the "minds, bodies, and souls" of the children in the classroom. Then, once we have found the answer, we **must** assume the responsibility of insuring that it's not Huxley's happy "slavery," but rather **freedom** that our children and grandchildren will enjoy.

In the late 1980's, the U.S. Department of Labor and the U.S. Department of Education (with the encouragement of big business) came together to identify what skills are necessary to produce a good worker. The foundation was laid for the 1992 report, Secretary's Commission on Achieving Necessary Skills (SCANS), "Learning A Living, A Blueprint for High Performance." This report defined the students as "human resources [to be] develop[ed]"[8] by a partnership of the government and business, for the use by the state. Central to the entire process is that government bureaucrats will determine future job needs such as how many welders or how many brain surgeons, etc., will be needed 20 years in the future. The School-to-Work Opportunities bill (S 1361) was based on the 1992 SCANS report.

> ## STWO is not just a job training program, it is centralized control of the labor market, starting at the schoolhouse.

Missouri's educational reform bill in the 1990s, SB 380, mandated "Beginning July 1, 1994, the director of the division of employment security of the department of labor and industrial relations shall provide annually to the commissioner of education a listing of demand occupations in the state including sub-state projections."[9] This is in line with the SCANS report and School-to-Work which allowed states to "expend funds" for "providing labor market information to local partnerships that is useful in determining which high-skill, high-wage occupations are in demand."[10] Although this might seem logical at first, this is essentially a key part of all totalitarian systems where the "commissar" sets the five-year plans, and the government dictates jobs, not the free market. It is the command economics of the old Soviet Union, not the free market.

Students Monitored for Life

"School-to-Work Opportunities systems" were to be set up in every state. The "activities of the program shall include matching students with the work-based learning opportunities of employers."[11] Included in the program is "workplace monitoring"[12] and "collecting and analyzing information regarding post-program outcomes of participants ..."[13] In addition, the bill included "linking youth development activities under this Act with employer and industry strategies for upgrading the skills of their workers."[14]

The tracking system set up is intended to function until retirement. "[A] national evaluation of School-to-Work Opportunities programs funded under this Act ... will track and assess the progress of implementation of state and local School-to-Work Opportunities programs and their effectiveness based on measures such as ... participation [by] employers, schools and students; ... progress in meeting goals of State, ... [and] outcomes for students in the programs ... which outcomes shall include ... placement and retention in further education or training, particularly in the career major of the student; and job placement, retention, and earning ..."[15] After all, educators ask, isn't it logical to see if education works by monitoring the student five, ten or perhaps twenty years after he leaves school? **The only problem with that question is that it assumes government needs to know and has a right to know all about you ... forever.** Bottom line? It violates a Constitutional freedom: "the right of the people to be secure in their persons, houses, papers and effects, against unreasonable searches. ..."[16] The National Security Administration has confessed that they are collecting vast amounts of information on normal citizens and storing it in a huge Utah facility. When the federal government mandates that the state shall "provide ... reports on the supply, demand, price, and quality of job training services in each unified service delivery area in the State" it stands to reason they will develop the structure and power to enforce it. Again, STWO is not simply a job training program; rather it is centralized control of the labor market, starting at the schoolhouse with the STWO legislation and continuing on into retirement.

Businesses Lose their Freedoms

An amazing assumption is made that all businesses will relinquish their control in hiring their employees. As far back as 1991, a proposed Oregon law had a section making the employer criminally liable if he hired anyone under 18 without the state-conferred "Certificate of Mastery," which was based on mastering a set of performance standards rather than completing a set of course work in high school. It was changed under pressure, but the attempt was made. The federal School-to-Work bill has built into it the enticement to hook business: "A partnership shall expend funds ... for such activities [as] ... recruiting and providing assistance to employers, including small and medium size businesses, to provide the work-based learning components described in section 102"[17] which lists how the money is given out. However, among many *mandatory activities*, Section 102 lists "activities developing positive work attitudes."[18] In addition, the employer becomes a part of the "performance outcomes and evaluation."[19] He will be a *partner* in assessing the "progress in meeting the goals of the State … [and the] outcomes for students in the programs …"[20]

Socialism Sold to the People

Assumed is the idea that people will not fall through the crack or that mistakes will not happen if the government does it. However, the Soviet Union's 70 years under communism gave the United States a real life example of how people live when their labor, education and daily lives are managed and controlled by the government – low production, scarcity of goods, long lines for basic food supplies, and impoverishment for the majority of its citizens. Are we subtly, by use of different terminology, being induced to adopt a way of life that will permit our government to control every action of its citizens? The choice of vocation is one of the primary means of expressing one's individual freedom to choose what to do in life, how to do it and even whether to do anything at all. How that vocation is determined will decide the extent to which the individual is controlled. Control of a person's employment and income is the essence of a totalitarian government.

Vladimir Turchenko, author of "The Scientific and Technological Revolution and the Revolution in Education," tells us:

> "The Marxist-Leninist principle of combining education with productive labour and polytechnisation of the school provides for a high level of general education and theoretical training. At the same time, realizing this principle to the full extent **demands a profound revolution in the entire system of public education.**"[21] (Emphasis added.)

Quite simply, School-to-Work Opportunities Act (STWO) provides for a radical change in traditional American education.

COMPARING TRADITIONAL EDUCATION AND SCHOOL TO WORK

Prior to the "progressive education" of the last eighty years, children went to school to learn how to read, write and "cipher." In colonial times, most children were educated so that they could read the Bible, understand their civilization, including its history and literature, and carry out practical mathematical calculations with algebra, geometry, and often calculus. Even as late as the 1880's children, up to the eighth grade, were taught great literature, local, national and world history, phonics, and mathematics, including advanced algebra.[22] Education was intended to provide the abilities, information and moral wisdom necessary for each student to develop his/her own unique talents and gifts in the broadest possible way. Once a child learned to read independently and had been taught scriptural moral absolutes, he was instructed in the best of western literature and philosophy. Furthermore, he was taught to reason logically so that he could become a law-abiding member of society. After a traditional education, the child could go in any direction, often changing vocations a number of times, e.g., from farming to engineering to publishing. What mattered was a solid foundation on which to build.

The period between the 1850's and the 1990's brought incredible change. It was the children, educated with such books as the McGuffey's Readers, who took us from the Pony Express to cellular phones. Their academic preparation gave them a base on which to build an entirely different world, a technological world, that no one envisioned when they were in school. The genius of their education was that they were given access to tools of learning and not put in a box, confining them to someone else's concept of what they were to be. Freedom to achieve was not limited by a lumbering bureaucratic system such as the one we have seen in the former Soviet Union. When in the 1930's, the United States moved away from traditional/classical education and began incorporating progressive education ideas in the classroom, the stage was set for workforce education. Foremost was John Dewey's idea of a "hands on" classroom where learning attempted to recreate the community in the classroom.

Workforce – The New Education Plan

From the 1990's School to Work Act came these admissions:

"The goals worth seeking can be achieved only through fundamental **systemic change**. The School-to-Work Opportunities Act provides the occasion ..."[23] (Emphasis added.)

"A Revolutionary New Approach to Education ... School-to-Work ... means significant changes in the way teachers teach and students learn ... It involves systemic **restructuring** ..."[24] (Emphasis added.)

"Experts universally agree that this job [schools meeting drastically different goals] requires **reinventing** elementary and secondary education."[25] (Emphasis added.)

STWO has as its goal "a new human resource development system." Its purposes are to provide an educational system that will "prepare the students for first jobs" and enable youths to "identify and navigate paths to productive and progressively more rewarding roles in the workplace." The purpose of education is changed. **Students and all other Americans become *human resources.***

"Human resources," incidentally, is a Marxist term coined in the 1850's by Hegel. It has become quite common in United States government and business usage and appeals to businesses that need competent, compliant workers. The author of the School-to-Work paper, Marc Tucker,[26] suggested to Hillary Clinton "a major proposal ... that has to do with government organization for the human resource agenda."[27] (See Appendix II for excerpts from Marc Tucker's "Dear Hillary" letter of November 1992.)

The law, School-to-Work Opportunities Act, makes "employers joint partners with educators ..."[28] and forms partnerships that link "the worlds of school and work among secondary schools and postsecondary educational institutions, private and public employers, labor organization, parents, students, State educational agencies, local educational agencies, and training and human service agencies."[29] Every facet of life will be linked together – a *seamless web from cradle to grave.* The outstanding feature of STWO is the structure and control that is being exercised by outsiders over the child's entire lifetime; not just when he is a student, but for the rest of his life.

As chairman of the Senate Education Committee, longtime proponent of workforce education, Senator Edward Kennedy, used his position to push HR 1385. (See U.S. Workforce System chart, page 81.) The structure necessary to produce the "skilled labour force for the national economy" is clearly pictured in job descriptions of the "National Workforce Development Board,"[30] the "State Councils,"[31] and the "local boards."[32]

At the state level, the **National Board** will be responsible for funding the state planning grants. The **State Council** will plan for an "integrated workforce development system, including the development of a financial and management information system, a quality assurance system, and an integrated labor market information system."[33] Incredible amounts of personal information will be gathered to satisfy this requirement. The law specifies that for those "to whom assistance is provided, the following information [is required] ... Economic and demographic characteristics, including the participant's social security number, date of birth, gender, race or ethnicity ... education ... academic degrees and credentials ... employment status at the time of entry into program."[34] (See "U.S. Workforce System" Chart below for the flow of the system.)

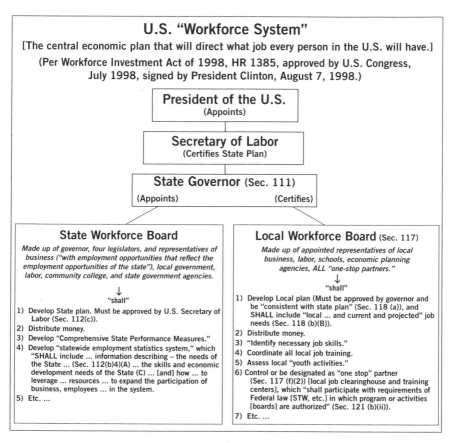

U.S. "Workforce System"

[The central economic plan that will direct what job every person in the U.S. will have.]

(Per Workforce Investment Act of 1998, HR 1385, approved by U.S. Congress, July 1998, signed by President Clinton, August 7, 1998.)

President of the U.S.
(Appoints)

Secretary of Labor
(Certifies State Plan)

State Governor (Sec. 111)

(Appoints)   (Certifies)

State Workforce Board

Made up of governor, four legislators, and representatives of business ("with employment opportunities that reflect the employment opportunities of the state"), local government, labor, community college, and state government agencies.

↓
"shall"

1) Develop State plan. Must be approved by U.S. Secretary of Labor (Sec. 112(c)).
2) Distribute money.
3) Develop "Comprehensive State Performance Measures."
4) Develop "statewide employment statistics system," which "SHALL include ... information describing – the needs of the State ... (Sec. 112(b)4)(A) ... the skills and economic development needs of the State (C) ... [and] how ... to leverage ... resources ... to expand the participation of business, employees ... in the system.
5) Etc. ...

Local Workforce Board (Sec. 117)

Made up of appointed representatives of local business, labor, schools, economic planning agencies, ALL "one-stop partners."

↓
"shall"

1) Develop Local plan (Must be approved by governor and be "consistent with state plan" (Sec. 118 (a)), and SHALL include "local ... and current and projected" job needs (Sec. 118 (b)(B)).
2) Distribute money.
3) "Identify necessary job skills."
4) Coordinate all local job training.
5) Assess local "youth activities."
6) Control or be designated as "one stop" partner (Sec. 117 (f)(2)) [local job clearinghouse and training centers], which "shall participate with requirements of Federal law [STW, etc.] in which program or activities [boards] are authorized" (Sec. 121 (b)(ii)).
7) Etc. ...

Notice the totalitarian language. At the local level, the responsibilities **shall** be carried out by "a workforce development board."[35] They **shall** "administer the workforce development assistance provided by all the programs [School-to-Work] in the integrated workforce development system in such area."[36]

Their job is to produce a blueprint that is to be incorporated into the "State Blueprint."[37] The task is carefully described: **"The [local] workforce development board blueprint shall –**

"(1) include a list of the key industries and industry clusters of small- to mid-size firms that are most critical to the current and future economic competitiveness of unified service delivery area;

> **This nation is being systematically stripped of its historic democratic values and transformed into a socialist state.**

"(2) identify the workforce development needs of the critical industries and industry clusters;

"(3) summarize the capacity of local education and training providers to respond to the workforce development needs;

"(4) indicate how the local workforce development programs intend to strategically deploy resources available from implementation grants and existing programs operating in the unified service delivery area to better meet the workforce development needs of critical industries and industry clusters in the unified service delivery area and enhance program performance;

"(5) include a plan to develop **one-stop career centers** ... including an estimate of the costs of personnel and other resources to develop a network adequate to provide universal access to such centers in the local labor market; ...

"(7) identify actions for building the capacity of the workforce development system in the **unified service delivery area**; and

"(8) report on the level and recent changes in earned income of workers in the local labor market, in relation to State and national levels, by occupation and industry."[38] (Emphasis added.)

A big bureaucracy is needed because each student will be followed by a mentor or caseworker (counselor) throughout school to insure that he goes in the desired direction. The mentor or caseworker is a government employee, not the parent, and the mentor will use a continuous teach, test, reteach, retest system to insure the student is following the plan laid out for him. Such plans are called IEPs, or Individualized Education Plans, and are put together by the education/government planners for the student by way of tests that reveal the student's personality, beliefs, attitudes, behaviors and work skills.

The Business Roundtable

In 1989, The Business Roundtable of Washington, D.C., an organization of CEOs from many of our nation's largest employers, committed to a ten-year effort to work with state policy makers and educators to restructure state education systems. They have been leaders ever since, using the Chambers of Commerce as their lobbying arm in both D.C. and in state capitals.

The primary goal in this "educational reform" was change. Jim Black, author of *When Nations Die*, contends "under this rubric of change, this nation is being systematically stripped of its historic democratic values and transformed into a socialist state, bound to the very policies and values that led to the collapse of the Soviet Union and others before that."[39]

DATA NEEDED TO MAKE THE SYSTEM WORK

All of this did not occur overnight. As far back as the 1960's, the vision was laid out in what was then the Department of Health, Education and Welfare. Using taxpayer's money, the department began assembling manuals or handbooks that enumerated every conceivable attribute of human life and translated it into a computer code. The data that was being computer coded included such information as "the condition of the soft tissue of the mouth," "religious affiliation," and "membership in community groups."[40]

What personal information is in the computer? If the individual has gone through the state employment agencies, his social security number, age, residence, education, and job aspirations are already in. The data banks also have the ability to document whether he "opens all [brain] receptors," "is a collaborator," or has "mind, body relaxation."[41] Or as Turchenko says, [has] "a positive orientation [attitude] towards the workers' professions."[42] The Department of Education report, "Promoting Grit, Tenacity and Perseverance ...,"[43] referenced in Chapter Five, brings Turchenko alive.

Certificate of Initial Mastery (CIM)

"... education is connected with the attainment by students of formally determined patterns of knowledge and skill ... the ... system requires strict controls for determining (through examination) an individual's mastery of established standards of knowledge and skill as well as ... so-called licenses ..."[44] Vladimir Turchenko

In the 1990s, the central feature of the STWO program was called the Certificate of Initial Mastery (CIM). In 1994, it was explained as:

Upon entering pre-school, the student will be assigned a mentor who, with the aid of the teacher and council, will determine what path the student will follow for the rest of his life. With constant assessment (of competencies, skills and personal qualities), the planners will be able to see what fine-tuning is needed, so that the student will fit into the prescribed job needs of the nation. His education will not be from textbooks, but rather he will be provided with desktop or laptop. His file will be constantly upgraded with information on the student's *physical health, nutrition, mental health, family, any substance abuses* and any other areas arising from the *one-stop-shopping* concept. There will be *lifelong*[45] monitoring by the state, using the file to carry the data. **Without this record, he will not be able to get a job or further education.**

In the ensuing twenty years, most of this has come to pass.

What happens to the student who wants to become a Catholic priest or a Jewish Rabbi? Will the state make those decisions? If so, what will happen to the non-constitutional concept of *separation of church and state?* What happens to students who are creative, but are unable to perform well in a formal, structured school environment? Thomas Edison, Winston Churchill, and many others fit this description. What about the inventor of things yet not dreamed of? Who will be his/her mentor or caseworker? Again, don't the errors of the former Soviet Union warn us?

Marc Tucker wrote the definitive work on the *CIM, The Certificate of Initial Mastery: A Primer.* It is part of the Workforce Skills Program located in Washington, D.C. Fully involved in the Common Core efforts, Tucker's 1992 letter to Bill and Hillary Clinton puts most of it into play. (See Appendix II for Marc Tucker's "Dear Hillary" Letter.) He opened the *CIM* with,

"The National Center's Workforce Skills Program is working to build a human resources investment system in the United States ... to create a single, comprehensive system for general, professional and technical education that meets the need of everyone ..."[46]

Tucker described his version of the history of American education, noting that:

"the most compelling ... vision [of the goals of secondary education] was ... John Dewey ['s] ... in the progressive education movement ... Dewey's commitment to the idea that fully functioning adults required a high school curriculum that was not the arid, elitist academic one ... but rather ... [one] that ... developed in the student the capacity to function knowledgeably and responsibly in an increasingly complex society ..."[47] "Dewey anticipated ... the subtle interdependence between doing and understanding."[48]

Tucker described the CIM: "The same standard for all – both thinking and doing." Since when has education in the United States demanded *same thinking*? He continues,

"The national system would be confined to certifying scores (and therefore certificates) for student's accomplishments in the core subjects ... and in applied learning. By 'applied learning' we mean the generic skills required to succeed in the high performance workplaces of the future, such as ... working with others; solving problems ..."[49] "The rubrics used to judge the quality of student work will be developed by the consortium of participating jurisdictions."[50]

(Tucker's consortium developed the Missouri pilot assessment, "Trash Troubles" discussed in Chapter Five.)

In addition, the CIM will not be limited to students, but rather will be "available" to "out-of-school youth, the chronically unemployed, and employed adults."[51] "Everyone would be expected to meet [the CIM standards], regardless of future career and education plans."[52]

The CIM will be awarded on the "basis" of the "New Standards [Project's] ... assessments."[53] All scores for the assessments will be "link[ed] ... to national and international benchmarks."[54] What kind of *benchmarks* are envisioned? Oregon mandated the CIM for all students. The legislation summaries cited for HB 3565, Appendix A, "Benchmarks Associated with the Integration of Social Services with Schools," list such items as "The pregnancy rate will not exceed 8 per 1,000 females age 10-17" and "100 percent of babies and toddlers will receive basic health care."[55] What kind of government force and activity will be needed to ensure this *benchmark*?

> Everyone would be expected to meet the CIM standards, regardless of future career and education plans.

All of the above information on the CIM was developed before Common Core and before the advent of all schools being wired to the Internet and students having personal computers tied into the system. Once again, it is an example of the totalitarian thinking of control from the top.

Who Will Set the "Skill Standards"?

According to Tucker, the "skill" standards will be developed by "groups of employers ... People meeting the standards in a particular cluster area would get a skills certificate ... At the top of this standards system, tier three, are skill standards for individual jobs and standards set by individual firms for the way work is to be done in those firms."[56]

A good illustration of standards to be set by separate industries is what the National Retail Federation did. Their president, Tracy Mullin, said, "The goal of the job Skill Standards Project is to help the retail industry develop better, more productive workers ... who will make retailers more competitive and more profitable."[57]

In 1992, the U.S. Department of Labor provided a seed grant to the National Retail Federation. By 1994, the National Retail Federation had a framework, which targeted "professional sales associates."[58] It focused on *personal qualities* such as "problem solving, teamwork, courtesy, people skills, listening, work habits, speaking, learning, cross-cultural awareness, etc."[59] These were listed in order of priority and identified as critical to the success of the sales associate. Next in order of importance was "applied mathematics" (number 14) and "reading for information" (number 16).

The National Retail Federation had drawn up a *profile*, which gives the individual his/her scores for each skill, the industry average and the top score of the industry. Once the standards were in place, the "skill standards should have currency in the workplace."[60]

What does currency mean? Simply that without the CIM, no one gets jobs.[61] Among those organizations participating in drawing up the standards were such retail giants as J.C. Penney, Kmart, Sears, Neiman Marcus, and the former Dayton-Hudson.

The occupational skills certificates would follow CIMs. As Marc Tucker puts it, "They should not be able to get an occupational skills certificate without first getting their Certificate of Initial Mastery."[62] "The preparation needed to earn the Certificate of Advanced Mastery [CAM] will include a professional development plan that will enable students to complete a program leading to the National Skill Standards Board certificate."[63]

A survey of state requirements for the CIM, CAM, and Skills Certificate indicated that *political correctness* reigns. One of the *core applications for living* required for mastery for the CIM is to *understand diversity.*[64] Caution is necessary today when a student answers assessments and surveys, prepares performance portfolios and responds in groups, because *all* personal information is ending up in a data bank, on a *portable* CIM or Skills Certificate, and in the hands of a potential employer. (See Missouri's Community Career System Chart below.)

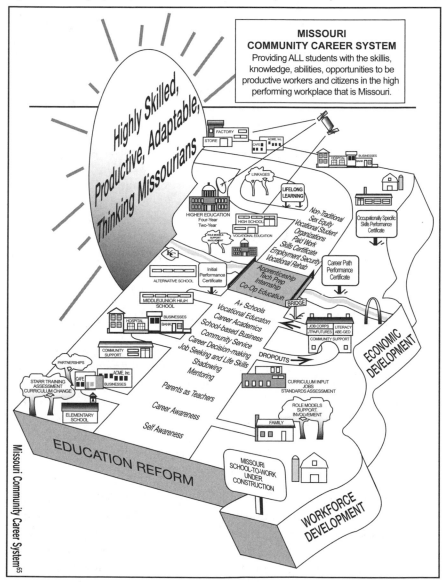

GOALS 2000

Background

In the mid 80s, the National Governors Association (along with several foundations and quasi-public educational groups such as the Chief State School Officers and the Education Commission of the States) and the U.S. Department of Education began to move towards setting national goals or standards. One of the federally-funded regional educational laboratories, the Northwest Regional Laboratory located in Portland, Oregon, began building lists of goals and objectives to be specified in the classroom. Initially, the goals were connected with the Mastery Learning movement, which grew into Outcome Based Education. That list changed from "goals and objectives" to be mastered on paper to "performances" to be demonstrated by behaviors, and now it is Common Core Standards.

By 1989, at the National Summit meeting in Charlottesville, Virginia, where the 50 state governors met with President G. W. Bush, a consensus was reached that the nation should pursue national goals, and start by identifying national standards. At the same time, groups of educators came together to select the particular standards for their discipline. Mathematics was the first to cross the finishing line with English, geography, science, art, and history not far behind. Once GOALS 2000 was signed into law, many of these people serving on the initial standards groups became drafters of the official federal standards.

The 1993 National Geography Standards

Standards did not just arise with Common Core. In June of 1993, the preliminary draft of geography standards was released. It seems that geography is much more than rivers, mountains and towns. Included in the Eighteen Standards are such words as *perception of places*, *Earth's cultural mosaics*, *economic interdependence*, *Forces of cooperation & conflict*, etc. The Eighteen Standards are supposed to flow into "3 Content Outcomes" as proposed by the "1994 NAEP Assessment Framework."[66] Included in these standards were such items as:

- **OVERPOPULATION**: "The student can analyze and propose plans to address population problems ... [and] devises a plan to address population for a region."[67] This implies that the student has the power to change where people live. Only totalitarian or fascist governments have that kind of power. The thinking behind this standard is the discredited

Malthusian theory, which declares "unchecked population increases geometrically while food and fuel increase only arithmetically." (*Essay on the Principle of Population,* 1798) This theory was proposed when whale oil was used for fuel, and crowded cities such as London had one of the highest standards of living. As such, it can hardly be relevant today.

States were already getting on board. Missouri's Draft Performance Standards stated under "instructional activities or assessments which [will] address the Goal and Standards: ... [that] students will analyze demographic and historical data from their locale in order to create a computer model to predict population trends."[68] "[The student] relates the planning process to the solution of urban problems such as employment, solid waste disposal, traffic congestion, high crime, drugs, education, poverty, stress between ethnic and racial groups, and air, water and noise pollution."[69] *This implies that centralized planning by government can solve problems of race, employment, crime and poverty, etc.* It is blithely assumed that too many people is the cause of these problems, and government action is given as the answer. The former Soviet Union tried this for seventy years.

- **ENDANGERED SPECIES**: Missouri's first draft of performance standards (required by SB 380, its educational reform bill passed in 1993) says, "Students will ... [e]valuate events, issues, and systems ... and predict their impact upon individuals, societies, and the environment."[70] The federal geography standards read, "[The student] can explain why the environment has limited capacity to absorb the impacts of human activity ... justifies the actions of governments in imposing laws that regulate human use of preserved areas and animals, (e.g., national parks, the bald eagle)."[71] Scientists are not in agreement that the environment is limited. Many have written that the environment renews itself and that most resources do not disappear, but just take on a different form.[72] However, the student is told he must justify government action on endangered species, totally ignoring man's private role in stewardship. Endangered species theories, as presented in textbooks, state that a certain percentage of species is disappearing each day/week/year. Yet, no one actually knows how many species there are in the world. Simple math says you cannot find a percentage when you do not know the whole. Little has changed when the proposed Science Standards of 2012 are examined. (See Chapter 4.)

• **EQUITY:** "[The student] uses data from developing countries to evaluate equity issues (... female versus male) concerning access to health care, education, and other social services."[73] What does this have to do with geography?

The 1994 National United States History Standards

"Those standards [National Standards for United States History released in the fall of 1994] will be the model on which school textbooks are written and curricula planned. The U.S. textbook publishing industry, as is its habit, will bend to whichever political wind blows over it."[74]

The United States Senate rejected the proposed standards in 1994. As the standards were enumerated, *The Wall Street Journal* noted, "In the world fashioned by these proposed standards, opinion and right attitude have primacy over mere objective facts ... [Yet the dates and facts that do occur are] of a select kind ..."[75] An examination of the proposed 2014 SAT and AP assessments show that little has changed in the history standards, except that now they are mandated if a student wants to be accepted into those colleges that count on the SAT and AP assessments to decide who is admitted.

In 1994, authors Gary B. Nash and Charlotte Crabtree, cautioned that "students must ... avoid 'present-mindedness' [and] judging the past solely in terms of the norms and values of today. ..."[76] Yet, as *The Wall Street Journal* comments, the standards for U.S. History place "insistent emphases on gender, race and class oppression."[77] A review of the front third of the 269-page book shows a heavy emphasis on the politically correct terms such as gender, *diversity* and environment. Under "Era 1, Standard 1" for the time frame 1450-1620, students are told that they should be able to "Demonstrate understanding of commonalties, diversity, and change in societies of the Americas from their beginnings to 1620 by: ... Comparing and explaining the common elements of Native American cultures such as *gender roles*, family organizations, religion, values, and *environmental* interaction and their striking *diversity* in languages, shelter, tools, food and clothing."[78] (Emphasis added.)

Former publisher of *Marxist Perspectives* and later Catholic convert, historian Elizabeth Fox-Genovese, was professor of humanities at Emory University and a member of the National Council for History Standards. She was quoted by *The Wall Street Journal* as saying that "the teaching of history implicitly means making choices: 'It means deciding what is important'."[79] The article notes "the theme of these standards is clear. It is clear in the remarkable degree to which the achievements of the West are minimized [and] in the politically loaded leading questions asked of students."[80] Many of the scholars involved in the project argued against the "anti-Western tone and general political tendentiousness."[81]

The 1994 History Standards failed to include heroes of the past years such as Robert E. Lee, Thomas Edison, George Washington Carver, and many others, but they do include a favorable portrait of *oppressed* peoples. One is forced to feel sorry for the *innocent, conquered* Aztecs, whose penchant for human sacrifice is not included because it is considered *unimportant*.

It is evident in Huxley's position on selective truth in *Brave New World,* that the 1994 History Standards are a perfect example of that selective truth. "Nowhere ... will you find any mention of the fact that it was the Western tradition that first produced the idea of individual freedom. Nowhere will you find that it was in Christianity that the concept of individual freedom originated ... you will find no acknowledgment of the fact that we have produced what no other country and tradition has," said Professor Fox-Genovese to *The Wall Street Journal.*[82] Even when the History Standards discuss the Northwest Ordinance, the profound statement concerning the need for religion is omitted.

The History Standards tell the students to "look to James Madison's letter to Thomas Jefferson .... [to see if] there was a need for a Bill of Rights."[83] Amazingly, the 1994 proposed history standards suggests that Thomas Jefferson had a hand in the Constitution, yet in actuality, he was in France at the time. The raging debate over the Bill of Rights was between Patrick Henry and James Madison in Virginia.

Furthermore, the 1994 History Standards are openly hostile to the Protestant Reformation. Under Standard 2, the student is told to "Analyze how *religious antagonisms* unleashed by the Reformation stimulated overseas expansion ...To what extent was the 'Black Legend' *Protestant propaganda?*"[84] (Emphasis added.) Most honest historians would not put the cause of religious antagonism in the lap of the Reformation and their *propaganda.*

Federal Control of Curricula

Technically, the Standards and Common Core are not a federal curricula because *federal law prohibits federal control of education*. "No provision of any applicable program shall be construed to authorize any department, agency, officer, or employee of the United States to exercise any direction, supervision, or control over the curriculum, program of instruction, administration, or personnel of any educational institution, school, or school system; ..."[85] Even IASA/HR 6 stated in several places that it did not intend to control curricula.[86] It did not, however, deny "exercising direction or supervision." But, if state plans must be acceptable to the Secretary of Education, including standards and assessments, then isn't it a very fine line that is being walked to say the federal government is not exercising direction? Indeed, we are being told that this is all necessary at the federal level so that a unified and "high standard" can be set.

IMPROVING AMERICA'S SCHOOLS ACT OF 1994

IASA established radical concepts such as parents and the state as partners in child rearing which means, in theory, that the parent is not the responsible person for the child's upbringing. Yet, in practicality, the language of the law **puts the state in charge**.

"... each school served ... shall jointly develop with parents for all children. ... a school-parent compact that outlines how parents, the entire school staff, and students will share the responsibility for improved student achievement and the means by which the school and parents will build and develop a partnership to help children achieve the State's high standards. Such compact shall describe ... the ways in which each parent will be responsible for supporting their children's learning, such as monitoring attendance, homework completion, and television watching; volunteering in their child's classroom; and participating, as appropriate, in decisions relating to the education of their children and positive use of extracurricular time; and [the compact shall address communication through] ... (A) parent-teacher conferences in elementary schools, at least annually, during which the compact will be discussed as the compact relates to the individual child's achievement;"[87]

Local Schools at Risk

The idea that local schools should not be in charge and that ultimately they are accountable to the federal U.S. Secretary of Education, not the local taxpayers is furthered in IASA. Picking up on this, Missouri's revolutionary education law of 1994 says,

"By July 1, 1996, the state board of education shall develop a procedure and criteria for determining that a school in a school district is 'academically deficient'." It then outlines the procedure for moving an academically deficient school into the "unaccredited classification" category which then allows the state to "attach to any (adjoining) district for school purposes by the state board of education ... [T]he territory therefore embraced within (the lapsed ["unaccredited" district])."[88]

Missouri has used this to effectively wipe out local control, local boundaries, and local districts in the City of St. Louis and a number of smaller school districts. Essentially, this means that school board elections at the local level can be negated at the whim of a state board of education that is an appointed board (in Missouri) and is responsible to no one.

State's Educational Reform Subject to United States Secretary of Education

IASA established that for a state or local educational body to receive federal funds it **must** have a plan that sets "content, performance, and opportunity to learn standards," and "opportunity to learn standards that address[es] ... the extent to which curricula, instructional practices, and assessments for students ... are aligned to content standards;"[89] It goes on to specify that each "State plan shall demonstrate, based on assessments ... adequate yearly progress ... that is consistent with **criteria** ... established by the [U.S.] Secretary [of Education].[90] No one knows what this criteria is.

**Common Core is the latest skirmish
in the *long march* to federalized education
and its accompanying thought-control. What
started in 1965 with President Johnson, received
a huge boost in 1994 and 2009, and is well on
its way to completing the Marxist vision of the
Frankfurt School. Truly it has been a
long subversive war.**

CHAPTER 7

REFLECTING A REVOLUTIONARY WORLDVIEW

THE CORE OF THE STANDARDS

*Common Core Standards are
fractured, lacking context,
socialistic, anti-human,
anti-Christian, and postmodern.*

REFLECTING A REVOLUTIONARY WORLDVIEW

THE CORE OF THE STANDARDS

A CAREFUL READING of the thousands of pages of Common Core Standards and the accompanying state assessments reveals the philosophy behind them to be fractured and lacking context, socialistic, anti-human, anti-Christian, and postmodern.

Fractured, Non-Contextual Thinking

Two competing concepts about teaching are at play. The traditional/classical liberal arts education laid down foundational truths and built sequentially, logically, and contextually on those foundations, ultimately creating an ever-widening knowledge base upon which any vocation or pursuit of life could draw upon and transition into.

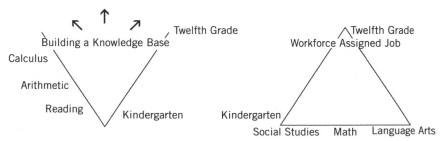

The second and the prevailing concept is most vividly reflected in the School-to-Work/Workforce Development model. Starting in kindergarten, picture the "V" upside down and start with a wide base of information with no context nor depth. (See illustration on previous page.) Then as the child moves on up, narrow it down until you fundamentally have a very focused and narrow point of study. Ultimately, the goal is to have the student choose a career in middle school and focus on that to the exclusion of the great truths of a broad liberal arts education.

The term *fractured thinking* is a way of explaining how the student today is exposed to so much information, exclusive of any context. Popular third grade social studies books start with the Pilgrims in New England, jump to President John F. Kennedy, and perhaps the abolitionist movement during the Civil War – all on one section with no logic, chronology **or** context. The next chapter does the same thing in the Far West. The child's mind then becomes cluttered with irrelevant facts that have no context and are soon forgotten. Fractured thinking continues in mathematics where building the factual base of arithmetic has succumbed to "discovering how and why 2 plus 2 is 4, or maybe 5?" Thus, the brain does not develop in an orderly way resulting in fractured thinking.

Fractured Thinking in English Literature Standards

Fractured thinking is on full display in the Common Core Standards. The full title of the English Literature Standards is, "English Language Arts & Literacy in History/Social Studies, Science, and Technical Subjects," and they are written for *all* of the areas mentioned in the title. Mixed in with great literature selections are historic speeches, scientific problems, and government publications. Selections for classic literature are numerous, but short. Although not a suggested reading list, so many are quoted that teachers will be challenged to choose which selections to teach, since their classroom time is limited. For English teachers to teach the Declaration of Independence along with other historic documents on top of their normal poetry sections, fiction, plays, etc., does not allow for the context of the Declaration to be discussed and taught. Already teachers are complaining that they have to drop Shakespeare in favor of the technical reading, since the standards specify more technical readings.

The standards give examples of readings to use to teach them, i.e., "exemplars." The choice of the exemplars seems to be random. Students are instructed to read out loud (without emotion) George Washington's Farewell

Address of 1796 and Lincoln's Gettysburg Address of 1863. Such writings, when treated as technical writings, remove them from their historical context of *what* was happening at the time, *why* it was happening, and

> **Ultimately, the goal is to have the student choose a career in middle school and focus on that to the exclusion of the great truths of a broad liberal arts education.**

who the players were. There is no time in English class to study the people connected to the documents and their worldviews. The historical readings do not tie into a chronological, sequential and logical study of history in the Social Studies departments, and because they are floating freely in time and background, the student cannot appreciate the context. Further, Washington's address is written with numerous biblical references, doctrine and alliteration, yet nowhere is reading the Bible even suggested as a resource.

The Presidential *Executive Order 13423: Strengthening Federal Environmental, Energy, and Transportation Management* is part of the eleventh grade English Literature Standards. Also presented as examples to study are *FedViews* by the Federal Reserve Bank of San Francisco, *The Cost Conundrum; Health Care Costs in McAllen, Texas*, and *Untangling the Roots of Cancer*. Eighth grade standards require students to master the "California Invasive Plant Inventory" based on the claim that "invasive non-native plants threaten wildlands." There is no time for a long work of fiction, which would more likely capture a teenager's attention than a dry plant inventory. In good literature, a good story line and plot pull the student through new and more difficult vocabulary words as the story context helps explain their meaning. Unlike government documents with terminology that has no meaning and which cannot be explained in the text, a classical piece of literature stimulates additional learning instead of contributing to boredom. The study of classical literature historically has been the platform for the seeking of truth and finding the answers to those questions of the soul, of the inner man: "Who am I, why am I here, and what is eternal?" Healthcare costs do not satisfy the soul or build character.

The influence of Frankfurt School's, Walter Benjamin, prevails in the standards. "The students are being taught that language itself is ... merely a conglomeration of false 'names' foisted upon society by its oppressors, and are warned against 'logocentrism,' the bourgeois over reliance on words."[1]

"The University of Arkansas' Sandra Stotsky argues that an emphasis on informational texts actually prevents children from acquiring 'a rich understanding and use of the English language' and 'may lead to a decreased capacity for analytical thinking.' Dry government documents such as those recommended in the Common Core's are 'hardly the kind of material to exhibit ambiguity, subtlety, and irony,' she observes."[2]

Fractured, non-contextual thinking handicaps the students' understanding of the world around them and prevents them from connecting the dots of cause and effect as well as learning to think for themselves. A national, non-partisan group of concerned parents and citizens, Truth In American Education, warns that Common Core "will prepare your child with empty skill sets and will teach them what to think, not how to think. Common Core will also foster 'teach to the test' practices."[3]

Socialist/Marxist

Does the suggested exemplar, Executive Order 13423, the *Executive Order on Strengthening Federal Environmental, Energy and Transportation Management*, promote socialist thinking? *Is it good to strengthen* the federal management? This Executive Order proposes to do such things as "reduce greenhouse gas emissions ... through reduction of energy intensity ... [and] implement ... sustainable practices for (i) energy efficiency, greenhouse gas emissions avoidance or reduction, and *petroleum products use reduction,* [and] ensure that (i) at least half of the statutorily required renewable energy consumed by the agency in a fiscal year comes from new renewable sources, and (ii) to the extent feasible, the agency implements renewable energy generation projects ..."[4] (Emphasis added.)

Did Executive Order 13423's climate change goal come from an August 2012 Executive Order mandating the private sector: *Accelerating Investment in Industrial Energy Efficiency?* Talk show host Mark Levin warned, "This is a fiat from on high for these utilities to change the way they process energy – an *enormous* capital expense and many of them are going to close down ... And they only have eight years to do it as part of this 'cap-and-trade,' and 'green energy,' 'climate change' bull****"[5]

As states start to implement Common Core, their departments of education provide examples of possible assessments. In Missouri's seventh grade math assessment, students are given an example of a word problem based on the socialist premise that government, not the individual, is the solution to problems. To prepare for the 90-100 minute, two-session task, "teachers must assign students the following task as an individual/group/class activity at least 3 days prior" to the performance task. (Notice that this is a **group**-learning activity – removing individual accountability in favor of the group.)

"Session 1 Analyzing Census Data

"You are a data analyst and are asked to compare local census data against national census data for the time it takes workers to travel to work each day. You will present graphical representations of this data, as well as any trends, to a county commission. The commission will then use the data you provide to make decisions about transportation needs for your community ...

"Part B. Mr. Jones is one of the county commissioners. He will recommend conducting a study *to determine the need for public transportation* if over 70% of the people your class surveyed travel 35 or more minutes to work. Based on your survey results, will Mr. Jones recommend conducting a study?"[6] (Emphasis added.)

The exercise ignores details such as: Did they all drive the same road with the same starting and ending points at the same time of day? The underlying premise is: *It is government's obligation to get people to work quickly by way of public transportation if necessary.* This task is not an **assessment** of math skills. Information is missing that would change the entire premise of the question. For example, public transportation (whether it is walking to a bus stop or light rail, and often transferring to different lines to complete the travel then walking to the workplace) almost always takes longer than driving by car. Also, it has to be subsidized with huge taxes to entice the riders. Regardless, the assumptions in the exercise are:

a) government **can** solve the *perceived* problem of taking too much time to get to work,

b) it is the proper **role** of government to *control* the people's freedom of assembly (movement) and

c) government can take money out of the pockets of some and give to others for a noble end (such as subsidizing public transit), even if the end *seldom* matches the promises made.

Socialism is reflected in another eleventh grade *Smarter Balanced* assessment[7]: Students read an *Environmental Protection Agency's Guide to Radon*, which explains "how and why to test for radon in your home."

Again, the assumption is that this is a *proper* role of government. The sample test guide notes that "the subject is very narrow and science-specific; some understanding of how homes are constructed, etc., would enhance understanding." This question itself is problematic in that this is for **English** class, not engineering, and there is little time to study housing construction. This is another example of fractured thinking of a science problem that is not in context.

Anti-Christian, Anti-Western Civilization

Science standards are anti-Christian, says Professor E. Calvin Beisner who reviewed the first draft of the national Next Generation Science Standards and the accompanying assessments and noted that the standards are *anti-human* and *anti-Christian*:

> **The NGSS reflect the environmentalist assumption that humans can't improve on the natural state.**

"A section discussing 'Human Impacts on Earth Systems' [which] says, 'Human activities now cause land erosion and soil movement … [and] [a]ir and water pollution … with damaging effects on other species and on human health. A later section, on biodiversity and humans, asserts, 'Human activity is also having adverse impacts on biodiversity through overpopulation, over exploitation, habitat destruction, pollution, introduction of invasive species, and climate change. The assumption that what people do is bad is clear in a draft of performance expectations, which requires students to 'provide evidence that humans' uses of natural resources can affect the world around them, and '*share solutions that reduce human impact*' as if human impact should always be smaller, not greater.[8]

"In short, the NGSS reflect the environmentalist assumption that humans can't improve on the natural state – exactly contrary to the assumption of Genesis 1:28's revelation of the mission of man: to fill and rule the Earth, not abusively but, reflecting God's own actions, in a godly way that enhances its fruitfulness, beauty, and safety, to the glory of God and the benefit of our neighbors. The underlying naturalistic worldview and the politically charged positions on Darwinism and climate change in the NGSS show that this will be one more step in capturing the minds of America's children – including those Christian children who attend public schools."[9]

Assessments are the Hammer

Chapters Five and Six spell out the incredible ability of the federal government and schools to track individuals through elaborate and extensive big data. The building of this data allows those in positions of power the ability to magnanimously elevate or maliciously destroy an individual. Federal agents will not only have the final say, but will be able to have at their fingertips immense and extensive information on **every American**, not just students.

Throughout the various pieces of legislation in the past thirty years, both at the state level and federal level, extensive funding is directed towards the assessment of this grandiose plan for *personal revolution in minds and bodies*, as Huxley calls it. In fact, *the assessment is the choke point of control. It is the enforcement.* The legislation sets up rewards for those who answer the questions the way the state desires and punishes those that do not. Henceforth, the state's correct answers become the priority.

Assessments determine movement from one point to another and are often open-ended with those grading them making judgements. With huge profiles created by the massive student data, a biased grader can hold in their hands the power to designate a student as either a doctor or a street cleaner.

Charter, Private, Christian, and Home Schools will be Controlled

Before there were even the assessments for Common Core, the New Standards Project of the 1990s developed the "multi-state examination system" which was intended to "drive the performance of all American students ..."[10]

School-to-Work states up front, "The term **'all students' means students from a broad range of backgrounds and circumstances ...**"[11] (Emphasis added.) The intent of all of the related legislation is to eventually control **all** students. The web that is being created will control charter schools, religious schools, and even home schools or if the child wishes to go on to college or get a job.

The word *public* is not included in the definition section of IASA. The key control of the student is the assessment tests that will have to be passed in order to be admitted to college or to qualify for the Certificate of Mastery that will be the means of securing a job. History has proven that if tests are mandated for future jobs or education, every effort will be made to know what is on that test in order to pass. So, if the tests include such slanted standards as the 1994 Geography Standards, Science Standards, English and Math Standards and the History Standards, and the 2014-15 SAT and AP assessments, along with various other *politically correct* standards, **all** children will have to be taught what is on the test. So much for choices in the content of curricula. Charter schools are obligated to a public agency for their existence and usually have to demonstrate their success with the same state assessments that all public schools are now being mandated to take.

Huxley noted in the introduction to *Brave New World:*

> *Great is truth, but still greater, from a practical point of view, is silence about truth.*[12]

Huxley wrote this in the context of how to create the docile citizen who is so happy with servitude that he does not realize that he is a slave. Silence about truth. That sums up the assessments and tests.

The shift from educating individuals to be independent, moral, wise citizens who can reach for the heavens and excel has succumbed to the totalitarian Frankfurt School's goal of compliant, pleasure-seeking servants of the state. The assessments are the hammer.

Will we heed the warnings of one of the 20th century's greatest writers, Soviet dissident Aleksandr Solzhenitsyn[13]:

"Oh freedom-loving leftist thinkers in the West! Oh leftist laborites! Oh progressive American, German, and French students! For you all this counts for little. For you my entire book [The Gulag Archipelago] amounts to nothing. You will only understand it all when they bellow at you – 'hands behind your back' – as you yourselves trudge off to our archipelago [prison]."

CHAPTER 8

SOLUTIONS

WHAT WE CAN DO

The battle over Common Core
can be reduced to a battle between
socialism/totalitarianism
and freedom.

8
SOLUTIONS

WHAT WE CAN DO

AMERICANS ARE RESILIENT, and when they are aware of the threat, they come together and engage. **There is hope.** Even though *the long war* for power to control America's future is being played out in the classroom with the battle over Common Core, the *push back* is starting, and the American people are engaging. The life and death battle can be reduced to a struggle between socialism/totalitarianism and freedom. Retaking education from the radicals means that Americans must settle the question:

What is the purpose of education?

Americans must come together and agree that: Education **should** strive to nourish the mind, body and soul with the moral knowledge of Western Civilization's Judeo-Christian heritage, unlocking the spirit and soul through the classical works in literature and the arts. Education **should** provide a chronological historic truth about our nation. Education **should** build a traditional knowledge base of mathematics and science that reflects purpose and order. Education **should** develop independent thinking and reasoning with logic and historical understandings with the goal being to create compassionate individuals.

Americans must understand that: Education should **not** assert that all people be treated as groups of oppressed victims. Education should **not** filter all curriculum through the lens of social justice and gender. Education should **not** allow schools to ignore and banish all references to the spirit and soul in favor of materialism and attempt to create a world of robots instead of human beings. Education should **not** have the goal to turn out complacent workers obedient to the state.

The United States Constitution enumerates what the federal government is allowed to do and relegates all other powers to the states and the individuals. There is no role **anywhere** for involvement of the federal government in education. It is the role of parents to be responsible for their children's education.

Training in Schools is Dangerous

Today's educational system is rendering America unable to protect herself against an enemy intent on conquering her. Foreign ideologies are increasingly being taught in schools. In a recent world geography class at Lumberton High School, Lumberton, Texas, a "schoolteacher allegedly encouraged high school girls to dress up in full-length Islamic burqas, and then instructed the entire class that **Muslim terrorists** are actually **freedom fighters.**"[1] (Emphasis added.) Training students through role-playing and with incomplete information about a culture so different from Western civilization is dangerous. An unnamed student reported that the teacher said, "We are going to work to change your perception of Islam."[2] Today, few curriculums point out, "Islam's public law can be summarized as elevating Muslim over non-Muslim, male over female, and **endorsing the use of force** to spread Muslim rule."[3] (Emphasis added.)

Curriculum content determines the worldview of future citizens. According to one of the Lumberton High School parents, "The controversial lesson came from a lesson plan provided by a Texas program called CSCOPE, an all-embracing, online K-12 educational curriculum used in 80 percent of the school districts in Texas."[4] CSCOPE is a customizable, online curriculum management system aligned with the Texas Essential Knowledge and Skills, similar to Common Core.

America is awakening to the threat, but all of us must immerse ourselves in the battle.

INFORM YOURSELF AND NEIGHBORS

1) Study and understand the foundations of America and what made us free.

• Our Founding Fathers innately understood the nature of man. They grappled with questions such as: *Who am I?* and *What am I here for?* Today, education's greatest failure is focusing on the material and the finite as spelled out in Socialism/Marxism/Humanism instead of the infinite and eternal found in Western civilization.

• Study the spiritual principles behind the founders of America. Emulate them by reading the Bible for wisdom and guidance. Equip yourself and those around you with *10 Steps FOR Freedom*[5], an in-home study that will equip you to become one of many Americans building a critical mass of understanding of the clear and present dangers to America, the blessing of liberty and freedom, and the hope of a better future. Available from The Constitutional Coalition.

2) Inform yourself on the issues of curriculum, state laws on education and climate of the local school board. Get to know your school's teachers and administrators.

• Many good teachers are just as frustrated as parents and would be thrilled to work with the parents to improve their schools. Cooperation rather than confrontation is the goal. When enough citizens begin to dig out the information from their own districts and states, and communicate with the teachers and elected school boards, positive changes can be made.

• See the list in Appendix III which includes names of organizations involved in the Common Core battle. There is also a link for helpful videos and books on curriculum, education policy, and strategies. Take time to learn about such subversive groups as the Frankfurt School and their war against America through the schools.

• Each person should check his own state's *reform* legislation and his state's constitutional education laws and requirements. Then, compare them to the federal to see where positive steps to bring the power back to the local can be made.

- One of the most liberating foundational principles of America is risk-taking entrepreneurship, which laid the basis for something called *upward mobility*. Upward mobility is a documented statistic of the poor moving into a middle class and a lower class having big screen TVs, cell phones, and the opportunities to better themselves by hard work and accountability for their actions. A look at the wealthiest Americans documents stories of many who became wealthy after starting from nothing. In many cases, the poor in America do not have to go hungry, physically or spiritually, due to America's generosity. Thomas Sowell's book, "Basic Economics," brings a basic understanding of the fundamental economic principles and how they explain our lives.

3) Get to know elected officials.

Make friends with those that represent you on your school board, your city officials and those in the state legislature. Share with them the information you have learned.

TAKE ACTION

Form a neighborhood group to start the reversal process through:

1) Revisions of state constitutions and statues that put mandates on local schools.
These include such things as mandated funding by the state tied to assessments and tests. The accountability must be moved from the state education bureaucrats back to the elected local school boards for all decisions on testing/assessments and curriculum. It also means revisiting the role of state boards of education, because many are unelected and unaccountable.

2) Walk back curriculum choices and testing to the local level.
At issue is **who** is deciding what is best for children. The nation is familiar with New York Mayor Bloomberg and his campaign to regulate the people of New York's personal decisions. As Glenn Beck said, "Bloomberg is the one deciding what the 'good life' looks like. Therefore, if you're a fan of fatty foods, smoking, sodas, bottle feeding infants, guns, Styrofoam, or the latest item under Bloomberg attack (loud music on your personal media player), you might be out of luck."[6] Common Core is, in reality, an unaccountable, distant, unelected, government employee deciding what the *good life* is for your child.

3) State legislatures must refuse federal funding. The first place to start is to do the simple math of what compliance costs the local schools as well as the running of the state departments of education, whose primary existence is enforcement of federal mandates. Although compliance costs may not zero out the federal money, it may be close. Furthermore, the freedom to ultimately focus on teaching, not mandates, and to plow the dollars spent on administration back into the classroom could change our nation.

4) Return to tests of knowledge like the Iowa Basics of fifty years ago. Reject assessments and the obscene costs of the assessment industry, computers and accompanying thought manipulation. Stand up to the enforcers and refuse to allow your children to be "assessed."

5) Encourage intelligent, morally strong young and second career people to enter teaching. Then give them the academic and moral foundations to do the job. Salaries can be raised if the top-heavy administration costs are minimized.

6) Remove the state from the Common Core mandates. A number of states are considering legislation to be removed from Common Core. In Michigan, the *Detroit News* editorialized in an article titled *Should 'common' be education's goal?* "… If public schools across the country are mirrors of each other, that's an **invitation to mediocrity.**"[7] (Emphasis added.) Recognizing this, legislators can remove the funding for implementation of Common Core components as well as pass laws to return the decision making to the local school board.

7) Continue to organize, educate and join with others. Meet with friends and family and talk about the ideas to which you are being exposed. Define your own worldview, i.e., what you believe and why it is important. Then become involved in your church, join or run for school board, help those of like mind run for public office, or run yourself. When enough citizens agree that the Common Core is not the way, it can be stopped.

8) Get involved in raising the literacy rate in your community, especially in the poorer areas. If an individual cannot read, neither can he solve word problems in mathematics and science; nor can he read the newspaper to gather enough information to vote so that he may remain free. He does not need elite groups making decisions for him. America was founded on the understanding that people have innate abilities. If they are taught to read, to discern, and to be morally strong, they can run their own lives, making their own decisions without a "nanny state" telling them what to do.

Arthur S. Trace said in, *What Ivan Knows that Johnny Doesn't*:

"In a profound sense the reading program is the backbone of the curriculum of any school system. Perhaps no factor more strongly dictates the success of a student's academic career than his ability to comprehend the printed page ... virtually every other academic subject that he studies demands that he read textbooks and other material – and he must be able to understand what he reads; otherwise he will be handicapped in school and in later life as well."[8]

9) Encourage traditional marriage of a man and woman. Solid
sociological research backs up the findings that a child does best in school when he is part of a healthy, **traditional** family as was ordained by God.

10) Pray for our nation. Pray for America, for others and for yourself.
Many will be challenged when taking a stand and will need prayer support. Start with 2 Chronicles 7:14: "... if my people, who are called by my name, will humble themselves and pray and seek my face and turn from their wicked ways, then will I hear from heaven, and will forgive their sin and will heal their land."

Man, through the cloak of government, must cease playing God with other people's lives.

OUR MISSION – *We the People ...*

In 1926 when Congress considered establishing a federal department of education, noted Princeton theologian Dr. J. Gresham Machen testified before a joint committee. Machen said,

"If you give the bureaucrats the children, you might as well give them everything else as well. ... Intellectual decline comes through the development of this principle of unification and standardization to which I object, for I think that in the sphere of education uniformity always means not something uniformly high but something uniformly low, ..."[9]

Every child has dreams and aspires to be somebody important, to be somebody that matters. Parents want the best for their children and work hard to encourage and enable them to excel toward their dreams. Bureaucratically controlled, Common Core stifles exceptionalism and chills the dreams. The spirit is crushed and the soul drowned, leaving zombies who are dead, but alive without souls, or robots that are artificial beings and slaves to a master.

Push back starts in the schools, but ultimately, if successful, **we the people** are back in charge, not the progressive dictators. *Push back* starts when we choose to speak the truth in love. Facts sometimes are painful, but facts not spoken are often deadly. We must speak the truth to all we know and care about. Most importantly, the bottom line is that **we must speak!**

Two hundred-plus years ago, a group of men took pen in hand and signed a piece of paper *pledging their lives, fortunes, and sacred honor*. What gave them courage? Most of them were biblically literate. Could their courage have come from the familiar Scripture,

> "For the weapons of our warfare are not carnal but mighty
> in God for pulling down strongholds, casting down
> arguments and every high thing that exalts itself against the
> knowledge of God, bringing every thought into captivity
> to the obedience of Christ ..." (2 Corinthians 10: 4-5)

Did these men grasp that their own strength and purpose came from being "endowed by their Creator" not only for "Life, Liberty and the pursuit of Happiness," but for eternity? That allowed them to stand and speak in obedience to God the Father, Son and Holy Spirit.

Can we do no less? For them their convictions meant almost certain death. For us, it is still just a risk of time and money lost. Dare we wait until it gets to the point of great sacrifice?

> "... 'Let each one of you speak truth with his neighbor,' for
> we are members of one another." (Ephesians 4:25)

> **There is a flickering spark in each of us, which if struck at just the right age, will light up the rest of our lives.**
> President Ronald Reagan

APPENDIX I

REVIEW OF COMMON CORE

Q. What is Common Core?

A. Common Core is the *latest* name for the nationalization of local education by United States government agencies and their partners (for-profit/non-profit corporations) committed to dictating top-down education policy. Prior attempts at controlling policy have been Progressive Education, Mastery Education, Outcome-based Education, GOALS 2000, and No Child Left Behind. Common Core purports to provide exceptional educational standards and assessments.

Q. Who is behind Common Core?

A. Common Core is the creation of two corporations: Chief State School Officers (CSSO) and The National Governors Association (NGA). Both of these organizations are **private** organizations with **no accountability** to either parents, teachers, or state legislatures in whose hands educational policy has traditionally been set. In 2009, they used their joint creation, Achieve, with help from *United States* *government stimulus money* as the incentive, to encourage states to sign a contract with them. They succeeded in persuading 46 states to sign *blank* contracts with *no cost projections* (a procedure required of all state legislatures as a condition of filing proposed legislation). It was several years later that the states began to learn what they traded for that money. Education is one of the richest sources of government money in the United States, providing money for consultants, publishers, computer/technical companies, and remedial educators. In addition, Microsoft founder Bill Gates and Pearson Publishing have poured millions into promoting Common Core.

Q. What is wrong with educational standards?
Doesn't Common Core just set the educational standards that every district needs to have for its students?

A. Standards are needed, but one-size-fits-all *national* standards that ignore *individual* differences and that are *mandated* by **unaccountable** distant parties with financial stakes in the game should not take precedence over standards set by teachers in cooperation with parents. With the federal government tying assessments to the standards and using federal funding as a hammer, it puts incredible power in the hands of people who have a *financial* stake in the outcome, **not** parents and teachers.

Q. What about Common Core curriculum?
Does Common Core have anything to do with the curriculum that individual districts use? There is so much curriculum out there, can't the local districts choose whatever they want?

A. History demonstrates that if the school, the teacher, and the state receive more money for students scoring at or above a mandated level, then each will do whatever it takes to move the students toward that score, including *teaching to the tests.* When the tests/assessments become the priority, the curriculum will reflect the tests/assessments.

Already, curriculum developers are advertising that they are **"aligned with the Common Core."** If they are aligned with the Common Core, there is little room for innovation or inclusion of materials other than those promoted by Common Core's standards and assessments. Bill Gates (in 2009) commented that the Common Core's success would be measured by how well the curriculum aligns with it. Inspection of the literature, math and science standards and assessments reveal *entire* segments missing or downplayed.

Q. Are the materials suggested by Common Core defective?

Don't the standards and assessments include such things as classical literature?

A. They do include some of the classics, but Common Core has changed the focus of literature. The standards (English Language Arts and Literacy in History/Social Studies, Science, and Technical Subjects[1]) call for 12th grade reading to be 70% informational and only 30% literary (see chart below), which replaces reading complete works of the classics. Since there is only so much time for class instruction, a thorough study of an entire piece of great literature will be a thing of the past. Lost will be time to investigate the finer points of reading literature, including teaching character through literature. Teachers without science, math and history backgrounds will now be teaching areas in which they are unfamiliar.

Distribution of Literary and Informational Passages by Grade in the 2009 NAEP Reading Framework

Grade	Literary	Information
4	50%	50%
8	45%	55%
12	30%	70%

(2008). Reading framework for the 2009 National Assessment of Educational Progress Washington, DC: U.S. Government Printing Office.
(From "Read the Standards, English Language Arts/Literacy Standards.")

As to the quality of the literature, already there are complaints from parents that some of the materials are X-rated and inappropriate for students. Missing is any study of the underlying foundation of Western civilization, the Old and New Testaments, and Christianity's impact on art, literature, science, and math.

In math, instead of building a knowledge base of facts quickly, time is diverted to understanding mathematical reasoning with estimations (or suggestions to "ask your neighbor") often taking the place of precise and correct answers. Much of the math standards and assessments is built around what has come to be called "fuzzy math." By slowing down the building of a knowledge base, algebra is pushed back a year, and ultimately, calculus and trigonometry are out of reach in a K-12 system. This translates into fewer students being able to handle what is now college math, which will ultimately affect many of their jobs. The science standards likewise shortchange the traditional sciences with environmentalism (man-caused climate change, etc.) and evolution taking a bigger role with the emphasis fading on chemistry and physics.

Q. How are Standards enforced?

A. Federal money to the state requires assessments that show a measure of improvement each year. It is determined by the Federal U.S. Department of Education how and what that improvement is. No improvement – no federal funds, forcing teachers to "teach to the test."

Q. Can't the local school or states revise the standards?

A. States are allowed to add only 15% additional standards, according to the Common Core contract they signed with Achieve. Yet in reality, because most assessments are nationally written and *controlled*, it is impossible for anything to be revised or added locally.

Q. If parents and teachers have problems with the standards, assessments and accompanying curriculum, where do they go to change them?

A. **Nowhere.** Neither the school district nor the state has any authority to make any changes, so there is **no** accountability to parents and teachers for what is taught.

Q. Is all the data collected on the student kept private?

A. **No.** The way the contract is written with the assessment companies and current federal law on students (FERPA), anyone claiming to be wanting information for research has access to personal data. Additionally, long-term (lifelong) data collection, known as "Longitudinal Data," has been mandated for years and is ultimately to be merged with data from the IRS, healthcare, tax assessment, etc., to create a profile on each child and their family members.

Q. What is the cost?

A. "Taxpayers will spend atrocious amounts of money on these non-proven/unresearched national standards, national curriculum, national assessments, national teacher evaluations, and a nationally intrusive database of all students/teachers/families ..."[2]

Henry W. Burke researched the cost of Common Core nationally and found that it could range in the next seven years from between $15 billion to $30 billion, and that did **not** include the costs to the states of "set ups and administrating a national teacher evaluation system and national student/educator databases." He pointed out that the states did almost no cost analysis prior to committing their states to the Common Core. According to Theodor Rebarber, CEO of AccountabilityWorks, "Missouri will lose $331 million alone on the implementation of the Common Core Standards."[3]

Consultants at both the federal and state level, their organizations, and groups have been the movers and shakers behind the changes in America's education. Many are idealistic and truly believe that if they can centralize the decision-making into their hands, education will once again be healthy. Others are not so noble, and see it as a position of great power, influence, and wealth. Failure in America costs lots of money. Over the past fifty years, educational failure has become a very lucrative business.

In 1981, when I first went to work in the U.S. Department of Education, its budget was just over 14 billion. This figure did not count the numerous duplicate education programs in the U.S. Departments of Labor, Health or even Defense.

In 1994, Congress budgeted $32 billion for the Department of Education. However, this was just a fraction of the amount (7%) that was being spent on education across America. According to Senator Paul Simon, who calculated the actual amount spent by private and public interests on education, the total spent was at least a half a **trillion** dollars.

By 2015, the budget of the U.S. Department of Education was $68.6 billion. Using Senator Simon's projections, education spending nationally would be almost **one trillion** dollars. However, Simon's projections were before Common Core and on-line assessments that mandate additional costs of computers and technical support systems as well as the Internet infrastructure. The cost today would easily be **trillions** of taxpayer's dollars. In 2014, Missouri was able to save 4.1 million alone by just dropping out of a testing consortium for a year.[4]

APPENDIX II

MARC TUCKER'S
"DEAR HILLARY" LETTER

FOLLOWING IS AN EXCEEDINGLY edited version of a letter written to Hillary Clinton following Bill Clinton's election in 1992. It was written by Marc Tucker, a key player in the educational coup.

The "Dear Hillary" letter is worth reading in full to see how over twenty years ago, the system that is now called Common Core was laid out as a way to direct and control all of our lives, from cradle to grave, through a command and control top-down workforce system. If what you spend your life doing both in school and later is directed by others with a system of enforcement, you are not a free agent. Few knew "the plan" as it has been presented, under the guise of "for the children," so who could resist?

11 November 1992

Hillary Clinton
The Governor's Mansion
1800 Canter Street
Little Rock, AR 72206

Dear Hillary:

I still cannot believe you won. But utter delight that you did pervades all the circles in which I move. I met last Wednesday in David Rockefeller's office with him, John Sculley, Dave Barram and David Haselkorn. It was a great celebration. Both John and David R.

were more expansive than I have ever seen them — literally radiating happiness. My own view and theirs is that this country has seized its last chance. ...

The subject we were discussing was what you and Bill should do now about education, training and labor market policy. ...

Our purpose in these meetings was to propose concrete actions that the Clinton administration could take — between now and the inauguration, in the first 100 days and beyond. ...

We think the great opportunity you have is to remold the entire American system for human resources development, almost all of the current components of which were put in place before World War II. ...

What is essential is that we create a seamless web of opportunities, to develop one's skills that literally extends from cradle to grave and is the same system for everyone — young and old, poor and rich, worker and full-time student. It needs to be a system driven by client needs (not agency regulations or the needs of the organization providing the services), guided by clear standards that define the stages of the system for the people who progress through it, and regulated on the basis of outcomes that providers produce for their clients, not inputs into the system. ...

The first [high priority package] would use your proposal for an apprenticeship system as the keystone of a strategy for putting a whole new post secondary training system in place. ... new system of labor market boards to offer the Clinton administration's employment security program,

The other major proposal we offer has to do with government organization for the human resources agenda. ... while creating an opportunity for the new administration to move like lightning to implement its human resources development proposals. ...

A seamless system of unending skill development that begins in the home with the very young and continues through school, post secondary education and the workplace. ...

We have a national system of education in which curriculum, pedagogy, examinations, and teacher education and licensure systems are all linked to the national standards, ...

The national system of skills standards establishes the basis for the development of a coherent, unified training system. ... It is a system for everyone, ... The new general education standard becomes the target for all basic education programs, both for school dropouts and adults. Achieving that standard is the prerequisite for enrollment in all professional and technical degree programs. ...

A system of labor market boards is established at the local, state and federal levels to coordinate the systems for job training, post secondary professional and technical education, adult basic education, job matching and counseling. ...

Create National Board for Professional and Technical Standards. ...

Charging the Board with creating not more than 20 certificate or degree categories establishes a balance between the need to create one national system on the one hand with the need to avoid creating a cumbersome and rigid national bureaucracy on the other. ... The bill establishing the Board should also authorize the executive branch to make grants to industry groups, professional societies, occupational groups and states to develop standards and exams. ...

The legislation would require the executive branch to establish a competitive grant program for these states and cities and to engage a group of organizations to offer technical assistance to the expanding set of states and cities engaged in designing and implementing the new system. ...

Develop computer-based system for combining this data at local labor market board offices with employment data from the state so that counselors and clients can look at programs offered ...

Executive branch authorized to compete opportunity to provide the following services ... apprenticeship systems, large scale data management systems, ...

We propose that Bill take a leaf out of the German book. One of the most important reasons that large German employers offer apprenticeship slots to German youngsters is that they fear, with good reason, that if they don't volunteer to do so, the law will require it. Bill could gather a group of leading executives and business organization leaders, and tell them straight out that he will hold back on submitting legislation to require a training levy, provided that they commit themselves to a drive to get employers to get their average expenditures on front-line employee training up to 2% of front-line employee salaries and wages within two years. If they have not done so within that time, then he will expect their support when he submits legislation requiring the training levy. He could do the same thing with respect to slots for structured on-the-job training. ...

Public Choice Technology, Integrated Health and Human Services, Curriculum Resources, High Performance Management, Professional Development and Research and Development ...

The issue here is how to organize the federal government to make sure that the new system is actually built as a seamless web in the field, where it counts, and that program gets a fast start with a first-rate team behind it. ...

In this scheme, the Department of Education would be free to focus on putting the new student performance standards in place and managing the programs that will take the leadership in the national restructuring of the schools. ...

Radical changes in attitudes, values and beliefs are required to move any combination of these agendas. The federal government will have little direct leverage on many of the actors involved. ...

Very best wishes from all of us to you and Bill.

[signed: Marc]

Marc Tucker

END

~ ~ ~ ~ ~

A complete copy of this 18-page letter was placed in the Congressional Record (E1819-E1825) on Sept. 25, 1998, when Colorado Congressman Bob Schaeffer read it on the floor of Congress. It is also available on Eagle Forum's website (www.eagleforum.org/educate/marc_tucker/).

APPENDIX III

ORGANIZATIONS and RESOURCES

National Groups Involved in Education
(Partial list. Many also have state affiliates involved in education)

American Principles Project: *americanprinciplesproject.org*

Concerned Women for America: *www.cwfa.org*

Eagle Forum: *www.eagleforum.org*

Heartland Institute: *www.heartland.org*

Heritage Foundation: *www.heritage.org*

Home School Legal Defense Association: *www.hslda.org*

The Constitutional Coalition: *www.constitutionalcoalition.org*

The Pioneer Institute: *pioneerinstitute.org*

Thomas More Law Center: *www.thomasmore.org*

Truth in American Education: *truthinamericaneducation.com*

State Groups

(From Thomas More Law Center with active,
accessible Website/*Facebook* pages as of April 15, 2015)

Alabama: Alabamians United for Excellence in Education: Stop Common Core in Alabama, *www.auee.org*

Alaska: Alaskans Against Common Core, *www.facebook.com/StopCommonCoreAK*

Arizona: Arizonans Against Common Core, *arizonansagainstcommoncore.com*

Arkansas: Arkansas Against Common Core, *www.arkansasagainstcommoncore.com*

California: Californians United Against Common Core CUACC, *cuacc.org*

Colorado: Parents and Educators Against Common Core Curriculum in Colorado, *www.facebook.com/pages/Parents-and-Educators-Against-Common-Core-Curriculum-in-Colorado/369263259855000*

Connecticut: Connecticut Against Common Core, *ctagainstcommoncore.org*

Delaware: Delaware Against Common Core, *www.facebook.com/pages/Delaware-Against-Common-Core/141637639346274*

Florida: Stop Common Core Southeast Florida, *www.stopcommoncoresoutheastflorida.com*;

Florida Stop Common Core Coalition, *www.flstopcccoalition.org*;

Opt Out Orlando, *optoutorlando.wordpress.com*

Floridians Against Common Core, www.flcommoncore.net

Georgia: Stop Common Core in Georgia, *georgia.stopcommoncore.com*

Hawaii: Stop Common Core Hawaii, *stopcommoncorehawaii.com*

Idaho: Idahoans Against Common Core, *www.idahoansagainstcommoncore.com*

Indiana: Hoosiers Against Common Core,
hoosiersagainstcommoncore.com

Iowa: Stop Common Core in Iowa,
www.facebook.com/StopCommonCoreInIowa

Concerned Women for America/Iowa,
www.cwfa.org

Kansas: Kansans Against Common Core,
kansansagainstcommoncore.wordpress.com

Kentucky: Kentuckians Against Common Core,
www.kentuckiansagainstcommoncore.com

Louisiana: Stop Common Core in Louisiana,
www.facebook.com/StopCommonCoreinLouisiana

Parents and Educators Against Common Core Curriculum in
Louisiana,
www.facebook.com/StopCommonCoreLa

Maine: No Common Core in Maine,
www.commoncoremaine.com

Maryland: Marylanders Against Common Core,
www.facebook.com/MDStopCommonCore?fref=pb

Michigan: Stop Common Core in Michigan,
stopcommoncoreinmichigan.com

Minnesota: Minnesotans Against Common Core,
commoncoremn.com

Mississippi: Stop Common Core in Mississippi,
www.fa*cebook.com/StopCommonCoreInMississippi*

Missouri: Missouri Coalition Against Common Core,
www.moagainstcommoncore.com

Montana: Montanans Against Common Core,
montanansagainstcommoncore.com

Nebraska: Nebraska Family Forum,
www.nebraskafamilyforum.org

Nevada: Stop Common Core Nevada,
www.stopcommoncorenevada.com

New Hampshire: Stop Common Core in New Hampshire,
www.facebook.com/StopCommonCoreInNH

New Jersey: Eagle Forum of New Jersey,
eagleforumnj@gmail.com

New Mexico: NM Refuse the Tests,
www.nmoptout.org

New York: Stop Common Core in New York State,
www.stopccssinnys.com

North Carolina: Stop Common Core NC,
stopcommoncorenc.org

North Dakota: Stop Common Core in North Dakota,
www.facebook.com/pages/Stop-Common-Core-in-North-Dakota/43107624365048

Ohio: Ohioans Against Common Core,
ohioansagainstcommoncore.com

Oklahoma: Stop Common Core in Oklahoma,
www.facebook.com/stopcommoncore

Restore Oklahoma Public Education,
restoreoklahomapubliceducation.blogspot.com

Oregon: Oregon Save Our Schools,
oregonsaveourschools.blogspot.com

Parents Rights in Education,
parentsrightsined.net

Pennsylvania: Pennsylvanians Against Common Core,
nopacommoncore.com

South Carolina: Stop Common Core in South Carolina,
www.facebook.com/StopCommonCoreInSouthCarolina

South Carolina Parents involved in Education,
www.scpie.org

Tennessee: Tennessee Against Common Core,
www.tnacc.net

Texas: Women on the Wall,
womenonthewall.org

Utah: Utahns Against Common Core,
www.utahnsagainstcommoncore.com

Vermont: Stop Common Core in VT,
www.facebook.com/pages/Stop-Common-Core-in-VT/569577429756265

Washington: Stop Common Core in Washington State,
stopcommoncorewa.wordpress.com

West Virginia: WV Against the Common Core,
wvagainstcommoncore.wvconstitutionaladvocates.com

Wisconsin: Stop Common Core in Wisconsin,
www.facebook.com/pages/Stop-Common-Core-in-Wisconsin/185213384959404

Wyoming: Wyoming Against the Common Core,
wyomingagainstcommoncore.wordpress.com,

Wyoming Citizens Opposing Common Core,
wyomingcitizensopposingcommoncore.com

Resources

Excellent background books and DVDs of *the long war* and the battle for America's freedom and how to restore America's foundations can be found at *www.10StepsFORFreedom.com*

ENDNOTES

TITLE

1. Huxley, Aldous, *Brave New World*, Harper and Row, New York, 1946, p. xii.

PREFACE

1. *Front Line* is a periodic newspaper that provides exceptional information on vital issues not often addressed in other media, including detailed voter information on candidates running for public offices, judges up for retention, and current issues in the Missouri and national legislature. The Constitutional Coalition, PO Box 37054, St. Louis, Missouri 63141.
2. Klein, Alyson, "Historic Summit Fueled Push for K-12 Standards," *Education Week*, September 23, 2014, www.edweek.org, (accessed February 16, 2015).

INTRODUCTION

1. Traditional Math vs. Common Core/New Math: The *standard* algorithm for multiplication is a traditional way to multiply numbers, honed over the years. It involves learning to carry, and it takes seconds once learned. One of its beautiful attributes is that it grows rather slowly in complexity when the arguments grow in size.

   The *partial products* method and the *lattice* method for multiplication take many more steps, are laborious, and often confusing. Further, their complexity quickly explodes when the operands grow in size. Common Core promotes lots of practice with non-standard algorithms such as partial products and lattice method, rather than focus on the efficient standard algorithm. (Prepared by Ze'ev Wurman (www.ieee.org) for the Educational Policy Conference, January 24-26, 2013.)
2. *Education Reporter*, "Controversy and Porn Pervade Common Core Curriculum," January 2014, www.eagleforum.org.
3. Beck, et al., (2005), "Chapter 10: The Muslim World – Primary Sources," *World History: Patterns of Interaction*, McDougal Littell/Houghton Mifflin, March 10, 2007, www.classzone.com, as quoted in *In Our Backyard*, The Constitutional Coalition, PO Box 37054, St. Louis, Missouri 63141.
4. Owens, Eric, "Texas public school students don burqas, learn that Muslim terrorists are freedom fighters," *Yahoo!News*, February 26, 2013, http://news.yahoo.com.
5. Korach, Bill, "California High School Promotes Hijab Day," *The Report Card*, February 3, 2015, http://education-curriculum-reform-government-schools.org/.
6. Ibid.
7. Ibid.

CHAPTER 1 – Common Core & Transformation

1. As quoted by Coulter, Ann, *Godless, The Church of Liberalism,* Crown Forum, a division of Random House, New York, NY, 2006, page 152.

2. EAGnews.org, "Bill Ayers explains the left's power is in schools and classrooms." *YouTube.* Online video clip, www.youtube.com/watch?v=Zt9d-eRFql0&feature=youtu.be (minutes: 1:02, 1:36, 2:08, 2:19, and 2:40).

3. Minnicino, Michael, "The New Dark Age, The Frankfurt School and 'Political Correctness'," *Fidelio Magazine,* Winter 1992, as posted at The Schiller Institute, www.schillerinstitute.org (Accessed February 28, 2015).

4. Ibid.

5. Ibid.

6. "Comintern (kəmĭntärn') [key] [acronym for Communist International], name given to the Third International, founded at Moscow in 1919 [under] Vladimir Ilyich Lenin ..." http://www.infoplease.com/encyclopedia/history/comintern.html (Accessed February 28, 2015).

7. Minnicino, ibid.

8. Ibid.

9. Blake, Nathanael, "Marxism and the Planned Corruption of America," "Cry Havoc" review, *Human Events,* http://www.crossroad.to/Quotes/brainwashing/2009/frankfurt-dewey.htm (Accessed February 28, 2015).

10. Ibid.

11. Ibid.

12. *zombietime*, "William Ayers' forgotten communist manifesto: *Prairie Fire*," October 22, 2008, www.zombietime.com, p. 20.

13. Ayers, William, Michael Klonsky, Gabrielle Lyon, *A Simple Justice, The Challenge of Small Schools* (Teaching for Social Justice Series), Teachers College Press, Teachers College, Columbia University, NY and London, p. vii-ix.

14. Ibid, p. 1.

15. Kimball, Linda, "Cultural Marxism," *American Thinker,* February 15, 2007, www.americanthinker.com.

16. Glavin, Paul and Chuck Morse, "War is the Health of the State: An Interview with Howard Zinn," *Perspectives on Anarchist Theory,* Vol. 7, No. 1, Spring 2003, "flag.blackened.net," flag.blackened.net/ias/13zinn.htm.

17. *Wikipedia,* Howard Zinn, http://en.wikipedia.org/wiki/Howard_Zinn.

18. Bawer, Bruce, *The Victims' Revolution, The Rise of Identity Studies and the Closing of the Liberal Mind,* Broadside Books, HarperCollins, New York, NY, 2012, p. 27.

19. Achieve, "About Us" and "Our History," 2013, www.achieve.org.

20. The Renaissance Group, "Home," n.d., www.renaissancegroup.org/documents/conferences/2009_fall_agenda.pdf

21. Bawer, Ibid., p. xi.

22. Ibid., p. xiii.

23. Ibid., p. xii.

24. Ibid., p. xiii.

25. Minnicino, ibid.

CHAPTER 2 – Changing the Purpose of Education

1. Gravel, Tara, "Doctor, school officials deny physicals were inappropriate," *Pocono Record*, Stroudsburg, PA, March 22, 1996, p. B-1.
2. Hocker, Audrey and Bailey, James, letter to East Stroudsburg, PA school following March 19, 1996, physical exam.
3. Gravel, Tara, "Genital exams needed, doctors tell school board," *Pocono* Record, Stroudsburg, PA, March 28, 1996, p. B-1.
4. Gravel, March 22, 1996.
5. Gravel, Tara, "Anger Mounts on exams of genitals," *Pocono Record*, Stroudsburg, PA, March 26, 1996, p. 1.
6. Ibid., March 26, 1996, p. 1.
7. Tucker, Susie, letter written at the suggestion of her psychologist, May 24, 1996.
8. *Encyclopedia Britannica*, Encyclopedia Britannica, Inc., William Benton, Publisher, Chicago, London, Toronto, 1959, Volume 20, page 134.
9. Merriam Webster's Collegiate Dictionary, Tenth Edition, first two definitions of "resource" are "1a: a source of supply or support: an available means .... and b: a natural source of wealth or revenue ...," p. 997.
10. *The New England Primer*, Boston, 1777, p 11. Reprinted edition available from WallBuilders, PO Box 397, Aledo, TX 76008, 817-441-6044.
11. Ibid., Reprint preface, p. 2.
12. *McGuffey's Eclectic Primer*, Revised Edition, American Book Company, NY, 1909, p. 59.
13. Webster, Noah, *American Dictionary of the English Language*, 1828 First Edition, C. & G. Merriman Co., as reprinted by Slater, Rosalie, The Foundation for American Christian Education, San Francisco, CA, 1985.
14. Hall, Verna M., *The Christian History of the American Revolution*, Foundation for American Education, San Francisco, CA, 1976, p. 615.
15. Mussatti, James, *The Constitution of the United States*, D. Van Nostrand Co., Inc., Princeton, NJ, 1956, p. 12.
16. Johnson, Paul, *Modern Times*, Harper Row, NY, 1985, p. 275.
17. Ibid., pp. 47-48.
18. Ibid., p. 225.
19. Ibid., pp. 638-642.
20. Dewey, John, "The Influence of Darwin and Other Philosophy and Other Essays in Contemporary Thought," lecture given at Columbia University, 1909, as cited in Phillip Appleman, *Darwin*, W.W. Norton & Co., NY, 1970, p. 393ff.
21. Dewey, John, *Experience and Education*, Collier Books, MacMillian Co., NY, 1963, p. 18.
22. Ibid., p. 19, 20.
23. Dewey, John, *A Common Faith*, Yale University Press, New Haven, CT, 1962, p. 87.
24. Ibid., p. 31.
25. Dewey, John, as quoted by Nash, Dr. Ronald, *The Closing of the American Heart*, Probe Books, Dallas, TX, 1990, p. 91.
26. Dewey, *Experience*, p. 21.
27. Johnson, p. 228.
28. Reisman, Judith, *Kinsey, Sex and Fraud*, Huntington House, Lafayette LA, 1990, p. 2.
29. Zimbardo, Ebbeson and Maslach, *Influencing Attitudes and Changing Behavior*, Addison-Wesley, 1977, p. 89, as quoted by Reisman, p. 9.

30. Ibid., p. 5.
31. Reisman, ibid., p. 123.
32. Hefner, Christine, *Sexuality and Medicine*, Volume II, Reidel Publishing Co., 1987, Foreword, as quoted by Reisman, p. 4.
33. *SIECUS Report*, May-June 1982, p. 6, as quoted by Reisman, p. 130.
34. Sasse, Connie R., *Person to Person*, Charles A. Bennett Co., Inc., Peoria, IL, p. 212.
35. Ibid.
36. Ibid., p. 276.
37. Ibid., p. 274.
38. Ibid.
39. Ibid., p. 277.
40. Amiel, Henri-Frederic, *Bartlett's Familiar Quotations*, Little Brown and Company, Seventh Printing, Fifteenth Edition, p. 580.
41. Simon, Sidney B., Leland W. Howe, Howard Kirschenbaum, *Values Clarification*, Dodd, Mead and Co., NY, 1972, pp. 16-19.
42. Bloom, Allan, *The Closing of the American Mind*, Simon & Schuster, NY, 1987, p. 25.
43. Huxley, Aldous, *Brave New World*, Harper and Row, New York, 1946, p. xii.
44. Sanandaji, Nima, "High Confidence Not Translating to High Math Scores for American and European Students," *New Geography*, July 25, 2013.
45. Archer, Jeff, "Summit to Issue Call for Service in Name of Youth," *Education Week*, April 23, 1997, p. 1.
46. Grigg, William., "Compassion Fascism," *The New American*, Appleton, WI, June 9, 1997, p. 21.
47. Gravel, Tara, "Genital exams needed, doctors tell school board," *Pocono Record*, March 28, 1996, p. B-1.
48. Ibid.
49. Hocker, Bailey letter to East Stroudsburg school board, March 1996.
50. Matthews, Timothy, as posted by Ed Noor, "The Frankfurt School: Conspiracy to Corrupt," *Snippits and Snappats*, http://snippits-and-slappits.blogspot.com/, May 23, 2009, (Accessed February 28, 2015).

CHAPTER 3 – The Standards

1. Huxley, Aldous, *Brave New World*, Harper and Row, New York, 1946, p. xii.
2. Minnicino, Michael, "The New Dark Age, The Frankfurt School and 'Political Correctness'," *Fidelio Magazine*, Winter 1992, as posted at The Schiller Institute, http://www.schillerinstitute.org (Accessed February 28, 2015).
3. Robbins, Jane, "Common Core Hurts Education, Biblical Knowledge," *The Christian Post*, CP Politics, July 19, 2013, www.christianpost.com.
4. "Read the Standards; English Language Arts Standards," CCSS.ELA-LITERACY.L.7.5.A *Common Core State Standards Initiative*, www.corestandards.org/ELA-Literacy/L/7/5/a/.
5. Ibid., CCSS.ELA-LITERACY.RL.9-10.9, www.corestandards.org/ELA-Literacy/RL/9-10/9/.
6. Lutzer, Erwin W., "When A Nation Forgets God: 7 Lessons We Must Learn from Nazi Germany," Moody Publishers, Chicago, IL, 2010, p. 10.
7. Huxley, *Brave New World*, p. xii.

8. Perkins, Tony, "New History Curriculum: A Blast to the Past?," *Washington Update*, Family Research Council, September 3, 2014, www.frc.org.

9. Robbins, Jane and Larry Krieger, "The College Board's Attack on American History," *Breitbart.com*, May 28, 2014, www.breitbart.com.

10. Levy, Pema, "What's Driving Conservatives Mad About the New AP History Course," *Newsweek,* August 14, 2014, www.newsweek.com.

11. Krieger, Larry, "History abridged – New AP curriculum troubling," *Orange County Register*, August 18, 2014, www.ocregister.com.

12. Daniels, Kit, "Sixth Grade Assignment: Destroy the Bill of Rights," Alex Jones' *INFOWARS.com*, October 8, 2013, www.infowars.com.

13. Eowyn, Dr., "Common Core workbook teaches 2nd Amendment pertains only to REGISTERED ARMS," *D.C. Clothesline*, March 29, 2014, www.dcclothesline.com.

14. Spencer, Robert, "US Muslim computer expert running Islamic State's social media campaign," *Jihad Watch*, September 4, 2014, www.jihadwatch.org.

15. Scott, Larissa, "Stealth Islamic Propaganda Shown to Six Million American Students," *American Thinker*, May 25, 2012, www.americanthinker.com.

16. Ibid.

17. Spencer, Robert, "Photo: Australian jihadi's son, age 7, holds severed head," *Jihad Watch*, August 10, 2014, www.jihadwatch.org.

18. "Teaching to Kill: The Islamic State's Jihad Camps for Kids," *The Clarion Project*, August 28, 2014, www.clarionproject.org.

19. Matthews, Timothy, "The Frankfurt School: Conspiracy to Corrupt," *Catholic Insight*, March 2009, posted by Sean Gabb, January 18, 2013, http://libertarianalliance. wordpress.com (Accessed March 1, 2015)

CHAPTER 4 – The Science Standards

1. Coffman, Michael, Environmental Perspectives, Incorporated, 6 Heather Road, Bangor, ME 04401, 207-945-9878, www.epi-us.com.

2. Project Global 2000: *Planning for a New Century*, New York: Global Education Associates, 1992, p. 2.

3. Sustainable Development Knowledge Platform, "United Nations Sustainable Development, United Nations Conference on Environment & Development, Rio de Janerio, Brazil, 3 to 14 June 1992," *AGENDA 21*, https://sustainabledevelopment. un.org/content/documents/Agenda21.pdf.

4. Sowell, Thomas, "Stormy weather and politics," *West Newsmagazine*, February 3, 2015, p. 3.

5. Kerry, John, "Remarks on Climate Change," U.S. Department of State, www.state.gov, Jakarta, Indonesia, February 16, 2014.

6. Beisner, E. Calvin, The Cornwall Alliance, 9302-C Old Keen Mill Road, Burke, VA 22015, 703-569-4653, www.cornwallalliance.org.

7. Coffman, ibid.

CHAPTER 5 – Mind/Thought Control

1. Huxley, Aldous, *Brave New World*, Harper and Row, New York, 1946, p. xii.
2. *Education Week*, http://www.edweek.org/media/gordonpublicpolicy.pdf, February 2013.
3. Robbins, Jane, "Subject: Re: assessments," jrobbins@americanprinciplesproject.org, http://www.edweek.org/media/gordonpublicpolicy.pdf, p. 41, March 16, 2013.
4. Alexander, Rachel, " Common Core: What's Hidden Behind the Language," *Townhall.com*," March 18, 2013, townhall.com.
5. U.S. Department of Education, Office of Educational Technology, "Promoting Grit, Tenacity, and Perseverance: Critical Factors for Success in the 21st Century," Center for Technology in Learning, SRI International, February 2013, Cover and p. 44.
6. Sunstein, Cass R., "Open Brain, Insert Ideology," *BloombergView*, May 20, 2014, Retrieved from www.bloombergview.com.
7. Ibid.
8. Ibid.
9. *BloombergView*, "Contributors," Retrieved from http://www.bloombergview.com.
10. Sunstein, Cass, "Individual Profile, DiscovertheNetworks.org, www.discoverthenetworks.org.
11. Cantoni, Davide, Yuyu Chen, David Y. Yank, Noam Yuchtman, Y. Jane Zhang, "Curriculum and Ideology," "NBER Working Paper No. 20112, The National Bureau of Economic Research, May 2014, www.nber.org.
12. Browne, Andrew, "The Great Chinese Exodus," *The Wall Street Journal*, August 15, 2014, http://online.wsj.com.
13. Iserbyt, Charlotte, "Beijing Journal: Personal File and Worker Yoked for Life," *The Deliberate Dumbing Down of America: A Chronological Paper Trail*, Conscience Press, P.O. Box 449, Ravenna, Ohio 44266, 1999, p. 294.
14. Miller, Joshua Rhett, "Student-tracking system at Texas schools prompts privacy concerns," *FoxNews.com*, September 12, 2012, www.foxnews.com.
15. Malkin, Michelle, "The data-mining body monitors in our schools," *Creators Syndicate*, michellemalkin.com.
16. Ibid.
17. Mays, Gabrielle, "Parents upset over game played at middle school," *Fox11*, January 31, 2014, http://fox11online.com.
18. "Report: Florida Schools Scanned Children's Eyes Without Permission, *CBS Local*, June 3, 2013, http://tampa.cbslocal.com.
19. Sauer, Mallory, "Data Mining Students Through Common Core: #1 Data Mining Software," *New American Video*, April 25, 2013, http://tampa.cbslocal.com.
20. McGroarty, Emmett, Joy Pullmann, and Jane Robbins. "Cogs in the Machine: Big Data, Common Core, and National Testing," Pioneer Institute White Paper #114, May 2014, pioneerinstitute.org.
21. Kamenetz, Anya, "What if You Could Learn Everything," *Newsweek*, July 10, 2013, www.newsweek.com/.
22. Ibid.
23. Ibid.
24. Ferreira, Jose, "Knewton – Education Datapalooza," November 3, 2012, http://www.youtube.com/watch?v=Lr7Z7ysDluQ.
25. Tucker, Marc S., President and CEO, National Center for Education and the Economy (NCEE), www.NCEE.org.

26. "Statewide Longitudinal Data Systems," U.S. Department of Education, July 2009, http://www2.ed.gov/programs/slds/factsheet.html.

27. Kengor, Paul G., "Worried about privacy? How about Common Core?," The Center for Vision & Values, Grove City College, July 22, 2013, www.visionandvalues.org.

28. Proctor's instructions "Instructions for Completing your Answer Folder," ACT Plan, ACTimproveyourself.org, 2013-2014.

CHAPTER 6 – Setting the Stage for Common Core

1. HR-6, SEC. 1001(c)(6).

2. Ibid.

3. Title I, "SEC. 101(c)(3)," Public Law 103-382, October 20, 1994, 108 STAT. 3520.

4. Huxley, Aldous, *Brave New World*, Harper and Row, New York 1946, p. xiii.

5. Ibid., p. xii.

6. Ibid., p. xiii.

7. Ibid., p. x.

8. Learning a Living, A SCANS REPORT FOR AMERICA 2000, Executive Summary, U.S. Dept. of Labor, April 1992, p. 1.

9. Missouri's SB 380 SEC 16(3).

10. S. 1361 SEC. 212(f)(4).

11. S. 1361, (Report No 103-179) SEC 104(1).

12. Ibid., SEC. 102(a)(3).

13. Ibid., SEC. 104(6).

14. Ibid., (7).

15. Ibid., TITLE VI, SEC, 402(a) and (b).

16. Amendment to the U.S. Constitution, Article IV.

17. S. 1361, ibid., Subtitle B, SEC. 212(h)(2)(A).

18. Ibid., SEC. 102(a)(3 &4).

19. Ibid., SEC. 402(a).

20. Ibid.

21. Turchenko, Vladimir, *The Scientific and Technological Revolution and the Revolution in Education*, Translated from the Russian by Kristine and John Bushnell, Progress Publishers, Union of Soviet Socialist Republics, T-10504-991/014(01)-76 956-75, First Printing, 1976, p. 115.

22. See *Ray's New Higher Arithmetic* and *McGuffey's Readers* for content. *Ray's New Higher Arithmetic* is available from Mott Media, Fenton, Michigan. Originally published in 1880, over 120 million copies were printed. *McGuffey's Eclectic Readers*, Revised Edition was published in 1879. The fifth reader contains selections from Shakespeare's *Hamlet*, James Fenimore Cooper's *The Pilot*, poems from Longfellow, Tennyson and numerous passages from the Bible. It was published by the American Book Company, New York, and millions were printed.

23. Tucker, Marc S., *A School-to-Work Transition System for the United States*, from the condensed version of a paper prepared for the National Governors' Association, Publication Department, National Center for Education and the Economy, Rochester, NY, 1994, p. 18.

24. *pkickbush, Creating a School-to-Work Opportunities System*, www.ed.gov, August 3, 1994, p. 1.

25. SCANS Report, *Learning a Living: A Blueprint for High Performance,* U.S. Department of Labor, April 1992, p. xvi.
26. Tucker, Marc S., President and CEO, National Center for Education and the Economy (NCEE), www.NCEE.org.
27. Tucker, Marc S., "Dear Hillary Letter," November 11, 1992, Congressional Record (E1819-E1825) on Sept. 25, 1998, p. CRE 1820.
28. Public Law 103-239, Sec 3.(a)(3).
29. Ibid., Sec. 3 (a)(6).
30. "Workforce Development Act," 104th Congress, 1st Session, S.180, U.S. Senate, January 9, 1995, by Mr. Ted Kennedy, Sec. 4(6).
31. Ibid., (8).
32. Ibid., (11).
33. Ibid., Sec. 203(a).
34. Ibid., Sec. 204(b).
35. Ibid., Title V-Sec. 231(a).
36. Ibid.
37. Ibid., Sec. 232(a)
38. Ibid., (b).
39. Black, Jim Nelson, *When Nations Die,* Tyndale House Publishers, Inc., Wheaton, IL, 1994, p. 7.
40. National Center for Education Statistics, "A Handbook of Standard Terminology and Guide to Recording and Reporting Information About Educational Technology, Handbook X," p. 63., and "Standard Terminology and Guide for Managing Student Data in Elementary and Secondary Schools, Community/Junior Colleges, and Adult Education, Handbook V," revised 1974, 1993, pp. 30, 31 and 45.
41. Staff pass-out in Indiana Accelerated Learning Workshop, October, 1991, taken from *Workforce Exchange,* The Center for Accelerated Learning, Wisconsin.
42. Turchenko, ibid., p. 116.
43. U.S. Department of Education, Office of Educational Technology, "Promoting Grit, Tenacity, and Perseverance: Critical Factors for Success in the 21st Century," Center for Technology in Learning, SRI International, February 2013, Cover and p. 44.
44. Turchenko, ibid., p. 21.
45. Public Law 103-227 [GOALS 2000] TITLE IX PART I SEC. 991(d).
46. Tucker, Marc S., *The Certificate of Initial Mastery: A Primer, National Center on Education and the Economy,* April 1994, inside cover page.
47. Ibid., p. 2.
48. Ibid., p. 5.
49. Ibid., p. 8.
50. Ibid., p. 9.
51. Ibid.
52. Ibid., p. 10.
53. Ibid., p. 11.
54. Ibid.
55. Oregon Department of Education, Summaries of HB 3565, p. 53.
56. Tucker, Certificate ..., ibid, p. 10.
57. National Retail Federation, "Raising Retail Standards," Washington, DC, p. 2.
58. Ibid., p. 13.
59. Ibid., p. 25.

60. Ibid., p. 26.
61. "Only high school students who have a referral card from the Mercer County School-Business Partnership will be considered for work," *The Herald*, Sharon, PA, May 1, 1993, p. 1.
62. Tucker, The Certificate of Initial Mastery: A Primer ..., ibid., p. 16.
63. Ibid., p. 15.
64. Rothman, Robert, "The Certificate of Initial Mastery," *Educational Leadership*, May 1995, p. 44.
65. Missouri Community Career System, Missouri Department of Elementary and Secondary Education, Conference, May 4, 1995.
66. National Geography Standards by the Geography Education Standards Project.
67. Ibid., p. 30.
68. Draft 3, Goal 3, Feb. 28, 1994, Performance Standards, Missouri.
69. Ibid., p. 36.
70. Missouri Performance Standards Draft, January 14, 1994, p. 8.
71. National Geography Standards, Draft, June 30, 1993, p. 26.
72. Beisner, E. Calvin, "Evangelical Environmental Declaration Seeks Consensus on Controversial Views," November 1993, www.cornwallalliance.org.
73. National Geography Standards, ibid., p. 38.
74. "McCarthy, Seneca Falls and history," *The Wall Street Journal*, Eastern edition, December 30, 1994, p. A6.
75. Ibid.
76. National Standards for United States History, National Center for History in the Schools, University of California, Los Angeles, Table of Contents.
77. "McCarthy, Seneca Falls ..., ibid.
78. National Standards for United States History, p. 40.
79. "McCarthy, Seneca Falls ...," ibid.
80. Ibid.
81. Ibid.
82. Ibid.
83. National Standards for United States History, p. 87.
84. Ibid., p. 47.
85. 20 s 1232a. United States Code, Chapter 31, Education-Administration of Programs, p. 853.
86. HR-6, SEC. 1111(e)(f).
87. Public Law 103-382-Oct. 20 1994 108 STAT.3552 TITLE I SEC. 1118(d)(1) and (2).
88. Section 162.821 RSMo as amended by Section 10 of SB 380.
89. HR-6 SEC. 1111 (1)(b)(ii)(IV).
90. SEC. 1111(2)(A)and(B)(i).

CHAPTER 7 – Reflecting a Revolutionary Worldview

1. Minnicino, Michael, "The New Dark Age, The Frankfurt School and 'Political Correctness'," Fidelio Magazine, Winter 1992, as posted at The Schiller Institute, http://www.schillerinstitute.org (Accessed February 28, 2015).
2. Burke, Lindsey M., "Why all the cool kids are reading Executive Order 13423," *Fox News.com*, December 27, 2012, www.foxnews.com.

3. Patenaude, Heather, "Open Letter to Parents of Public Schooled Children," Truth in American Education, March 16, 2013, truthinamericaneducation.com.

4. "GPO U.S. Government Printing Office," Presidential Documents, Executive Order 13423, January 24, 2007, http://www.gpo.gov/fdsys/pkg/FR-2007-01-26/pdf/07-374.pdf

5. Adams, Becket, "President Obama Issues Major 'Green Energy' Executive Order," *The Blaze*, September 3, 2012, www.theblaze.com.

6. Missouri Department of Elementary and Secondary Education, "SMARTER Balanced Assessment 7th Grade Mathematics," n.d., http://dese.mo.gov/divimprove/assess/documents/asmt-sbac-math-gr7-sample-items.pdf, pgs. 30-37.

7. Missouri Department ..., SMARTER ..., ibid, ELA.11.SR.01.10.115.

8. Beisner, E. Calvin, "Public School Science Standards: Political or Pure," Cornwall Alliance, January 30, 2013, www.cornwallalliance.org.

9. Ibid.

10. Press Release, New Standards Project, August 5, 1991.

11. HR-6, ibid., SEC. 4.(2).

12. Huxley, ibid., p. xii.

13. Solzhenitsyn, Aleksandr, "Last statement prior to his arrest and expulsion from the Soviet Union, *LA Times*, February 12, 1974.

CHAPTER 8 – Solutions

1. Owens, Eric, "Texas public school students don burqas, learn that Muslim terrorists are freedom fighters," *The Daily Caller*, February 26, 29013, http//dailycaller.com.

2. Ibid.

3. Pipes, Daniel, "Explaining the Denial," *FrontPageMagazine*, March 18, 2013, frontpagemag.com.

4. Owens, Ibid.

5. Hearne, Donna, "10 Steps *FOR* Freedom," The Constitutional Coalition, PO Box 37054, St. Louis, MO 63141, www.10stepsforfreedom.com.

6. Ritz, Erica, "Bloomberg's Newest Public Health Initiative: Earbud Headphones?," *The Blaze*, March 6, 2013, http://www.theblaze.com.

7. Opinion Editorials, *The Detroit News*, March 4, 2013, "Should 'common' be education's goals?, www.detroitnews.com.

8. Trace, Jr., Arthur S., "What Ivan Knows that Johnny Doesn't, Random House, 1961, p. 9.

9. Machen, J. Gresham, (1881-1936), "Testimony before the House and Senate Committees on the Proposed Department of Education (1926)," Center for Reformed Theology and Apologetics, http://www.reformed.org/master/index.html?mainframe=/christian_education/Machen_before_congress.html.

Appendix I – Review of Common Core

1. Common Core State Standards Initiative, Read the Standards, English Language Arts/ Literacy Standards, "Introduction," "Key Design Consideration," www.corestandards. org, (Accessed April 9, 2015).

2. Garner, Donna, email, February 27, 2013, "Important: Map of States Pulling Back from Common Core Standards."

3. Burke, Henry, "States' Taxpayers Cannot Afford Common Core Standards," *Education News*, October 16, 2012, http://educationviews.org.

4. Department of Education, Fiscal Year 2015 Budget, "Summary and Background Information," www2.ed.gov/about/overview/budget/budget15/summary/15summary.pdf